TRUTH ■ FOR BIBLE

Life
in Bible Times

The Bible comes to life

Timothy Cross

Day One

© Day One Publications 2017

ISBN 978-1-84625-567-0
All Scripture quotations, unless stated otherwise, are
from the Revised Standard Version.

British Library Cataloguing in Publication Data available

Published by Day One Publications
Ryelands Road, Leominster, HR6 8NZ
Telephone 01568 613 740 FAX 01568 611 473
email—sales@dayone.co.uk
web site—www.dayone.co.uk

Cover design by Rob Jones, Elk Design
Printed by TJ International

To Philippa, my niece

ENDORSEMENT

I commend this book, which will help the reader understand how the gospel of Christ was and is grounded in everyday life. Biblical meaning is brought out in a homely way through the daily 'sights and smells' of the Holy Land, together with key institutions of religious life brought to fulfilment in Christ. I especially appreciated how it might help people today relate their faith to their working lives, as so many aspects of how people made their living or cared for their homes are brought out. This indeed is the world into which 'the Word was made flesh'.

Revd Canon Bob Capper, Vicar, St Mark's Evangelical Church, Cardiff

Contents

Christians believe that the Bible is no ordinary book but the very Word of God Himself. The Bible certainly makes this claim for itself, for it states, 'All scripture is inspired by God' (2 Tim. 3:16)—that is, all Scripture is 'God-breathed': the product of the Spirit of God moving on the human authors of Scripture, causing them to write exactly what God would have them to write and us to know.

As the Word of God, the Bible has a timeless quality about it. It is eternal as God Himself is eternal. Hence it is always contemporary and valid, irrespective of the age and culture in which it is read. The primary message of the Bible is 'salvation through faith in Jesus Christ' (2 Tim. 3:15). The human condition being the same now as it was in Bible times, the message of the Bible never loses its relevance or urgency.

Whilst all this is true, the immediate context of the Bible is the Middle East, and in the case of the New Testament the Middle East of the first century. The Christian faith is a distinctly historical faith. The customs, culture and everyday life of the Middle East in the first century were very different from those in a Western twenty-first-century city. To understand the Bible, therefore, it is vital that we understand something of the manners and customs of the times in which it was written, and read it through first-century as well as twenty-first-century eyes, being careful not to impose our ways on theirs.

The following pages examine some of the manners and customs, traditions and occupations of everyday life in Bible times. We will consider how people in Bible times lived their daily lives; their work, ways and the things they saw around them. We will put ourselves into the context and era in which the eternal message of salvation was grounded into time. When we do so, we find that the Bible comes to life for us in a new way, our understanding is increased and certain puzzles of interpretation are demystified.

Ultimately, of course, only the Holy Spirit of God who caused the Bible to be written can illuminate the pages of the Bible to us. If the Bible is to come to life for us, the Spirit of God has to make us alive to the Bible. My prayer, however, is that He would graciously use the following pages as a means to that end, and that as you read this little book, the Bible will come to life for you in a new way.

Timothy Cross

Cardiff

Wales

The fullness of time

G alatians 4:4 tells us that 'when the time had fully come, God sent forth his Son.' The events concerning Christ occurred distinctly in time and space. As noted in the Introduction, the Christian faith is a historical faith. The setting of Christ's appearance and ministry on earth is that of the Graeco-Roman world of the first century. When we consider that world, we are forced to the conclusion that the hand of God was working behind the scenes, preparing the ground, for the time was ripe for the gospel and the conditions highly conducive to the spread of the gospel message. 'The time had fully come.'

The longed-for Messiah

The Jewish people had always been characterized by Messianic expectation. Their Scriptures prophesied the coming of the Messiah many times. At the very dawn of history, God had promised a Redeemer—one who would undo the ravages wrought by sin and Satan by 'crushing Satan's head' (see Gen. 3:15). As time went on, Almighty God revealed further and fuller details concerning this Messiah, such as the manner of His birth, the place of His birth, His substitutionary death and much more. In the fullness of time, God fulfilled His Word and 'sent forth His Son'—His 'anointed one' and agent of salvation. The identity of Jesus is crucial to Christianity. When asked by Jesus about this, Peter confessed, 'You are the Christ, the Son of the living God' (Matt. 16:16).

In first-century Israel, Messianic expectation was heightened by the fact that the Jews were under pagan, Roman rule. They longed for a Messiah who would shake off this foreign yoke and 'restore the kingdom to Israel' (Acts 1:6). Jesus, however, defined His Messiahship in terms of being a personal Saviour from sin, rather than a political or military deliverer from a foreign power. His mission was characterized by suffering, not power. He was a suffering Messiah—the cross was central to His mission. When Peter first heard this from the lips of Jesus, he 'took him and began to rebuke him' (Matt. 16:22). A suffering Messiah who would redeem His people by dying in their place did not initially fit into Peter's frame of reference—nor that of others: 'Christ crucified' was and is 'a stumbling block to Jews and folly to Gentiles' (1 Cor. 1:23).

Roman rule

To the Jews, Rome was a foreign, pagan, alien power. Yet Roman rule had many advantages which were helpful to the spread of the gospel. There was the 'Pax Romana'—the Roman peace. Unlike previous centuries of national disruption, the first century was characterized by a relative stability and unity. The Roman soldiers were scattered throughout the empire. They enforced the peace. The early evangelists could thus travel in relative safety by both land and sea, free from attacks by bandits. The Romans were also expert road-builders. These long, straight, paved roads furthered trade and were also utilized to further the message of the gospel.

The Greeks

The conquests of Alexander the Great between 334 and 326 BC had an effect which lasted to the time of Christ and beyond. Although Hebrew was the sacred language of the synagogue, and Latin the language spoken by Romans, Greek was universally known throughout the empire. Greek was the common language of trade. In 200 BC the Hebrew Scriptures were translated into Greek. And the language used by the Holy Spirit to write the New Testament Scriptures telling of Christ was … Greek, and *Koine*, or common Greek, at that. The Greek language is 'the most subtle and powerful language that ever flowed from the tongue of man'.[1] The gospel has to be heard or read and understood if it is to be embraced. The gospel was carried on the Roman roads and proclaimed and explained in *Koine* Greek. The early apostles travelled throughout the Roman Empire, often using the synagogues as a launching pad for the proclamation of the Good News of Jesus. God blessed their endeavours in a remarkable way and they 'turned the world upside down' (Acts 17:6).

Incurably religious

The Graeco-Roman world of the first century certainly did not lack religion. The Romans worshipped many gods. Paul was telling the Corinthians nothing new when he wrote, 'there may be so-called gods in heaven or on earth—as indeed there are many "gods" and many "lords"' (1 Cor. 8:5). But Paul then went on to affirm, 'yet for us there is one God, the Father, from whom are all things and for whom we exist, and one Lord, Jesus Christ, through whom are all things and through whom we exist' (1 Cor. 8:6).

There is such a phenomenon as 'the force of truth'. Truth is self-authenticating. The gospel rang true in the hearts of many and revealed the falsity and paucity of the religious fare Rome offered. The immoral practices associated with the pagan gods were well known and unmentionable. The prevailing philosophies of the day were Stoicism—'keep a stiff upper lip'—and Epicureanism—'Let us eat and drink, for tomorrow we die' (1 Cor. 15:32). The Christian gospel brought knowledge of the true and living God and the transformation of many lives. It had an attraction and authority which nothing else offered. Pagan temples were emptied and pagan practices ceased. Lives and communities were transformed. 'Therefore if any one is in Christ, he is a new creation; the old has passed away, behold, the new has come' (2 Cor. 5:17).

The downside of Rome

Whilst Roman rule had many advantages—on the whole it granted religious freedom to both Jews and Christians—as time went on, the darker side of Rome appeared. The Roman Emperor decided that he should be worshipped. Public allegiance to him was to be affirmed. A pinch of incense was to be sprinkled into a fire and the words 'Caesar is Lord' were to be uttered. Christians had conscientious objections to this requirement. Whilst they obeyed the law, their ultimate allegiance was to King Jesus. 'Jesus is Lord' is one of the earliest Christian confessions, and it contradicted 'Caesar is Lord'. Christians' refusal to say 'Caesar is Lord' often saw them being thrown to the lions.

'When the time had fully come, God sent forth his Son' (Gal. 4:4). The first century was certainly ripe for the gospel. But we can also say that the twenty-first century is ripe for the gospel too. Why? Because we all have need of a Saviour, for 'all have sinned and fall short of the glory of God' (Rom. 3:23). And the Lord Jesus Christ is still God's gracious provision for our deepest need. He is as able to save twenty-first-century sinners as He was able to save first-century sinners. He is as able to save those living in our sophisticated technological age as He was able to save those living back in the low-tech Graeco-Roman world. Christ is still the answer to our every need. 'We have seen and testify that the Father has sent his Son as the Savior of the world' (1 John 4:14).

NOTE

1   W. E. Vine, *A New Testament Greek Grammar* (London: Pickering &Inglis, n.d.), p. 1.

Tent-dwelling

It is good to be able to take a holiday now and then, and enjoy a change of scenery and recharge the batteries. My personal preference is for a holiday on the English coast, in a nice hotel, replete with en-suite facilities, freshly laundered bed sheets and a tea tray in my room.

The luxuries of a modern hotel contrast greatly with the dwellings of Bible times, as before the people of Israel entered the Promised Land and settled in towns and villages, their living was mainly confined to dwelling in tents. Providence saw to it that they were campers—never settled in one place, but permanently on the move.

The patriarch Abraham—the founding father of the Hebrew race—had a tent-dwelling lifestyle very similar to that of the Bedouin tribes which can still be seen in Israel today. He and his sons had a nomadic existence and lived in tents. Thus we read how Abraham 'pitched his tent, with Bethel on the west and Ai on the east; and there he built an altar to the LORD' (Gen. 12:8). Genesis 18:1 even describes a pre-incarnate appearance of the Lord Jesus Christ which occurred when Abraham 'sat at the door of his tent in the heat of the day'.

Between their redemption from slavery in Egypt and their entry into the land of Canaan the people of Israel lived in tents in the wilderness for forty years. God commanded them never to forget this, and so ordained the 'Feast of Booths'—also known as the 'Feast of Tabernacles' or 'Tents'—to commemorate this: 'that your generations may know that I made the people of Israel dwell in booths [tents] when I brought them out of the land of Egypt' (Lev. 23:43).

When we turn to the New Testament we note that the Apostle Paul—educated Pharisee and Christian missionary that he was—was also a trained manual worker. And his specific trade was tent-making. When in

Corinth, Paul stayed with a couple named Aquila and Priscilla 'because he was of the same trade … and they worked, for by trade they were tentmakers' (Acts 18:3). Paul was adamant that a Christian worker should be paid for his ministry. He stated, 'the Lord commanded that those who proclaim the gospel should get their living by the gospel' (1 Cor. 9:14), for 'The laborer deserves his wages' (1 Tim. 5:17). Yet Paul was flexible in his personal application of this principle. There were times when he thought it expedient to support his ministry through secular work. He explained to the Ephesian elders, 'I coveted no one's silver or gold or apparel. You yourselves know that these hands ministered to my necessities, and to those who were with me' (Acts 20:33–34). How did he do this? Through his ability as a tent-maker—skills he would have learned in his youth in his home town of Tarsus in Cilicia. Cilicia was a province known for producing the very best goats' hair used in making tents.

Tent design

Tents in Bible times were simple in their design. They had to be easy to take down and put up, thus facilitating the nomadic lifestyle of settling down temporarily in a place suitable for feeding and watering animals before moving on. The tent itself was made of pieces of goats' hair woven together to make one large sheet. The qualities of goats' hair are such that it expands in the rain and becomes waterproof, whilst, when dried in the sun, it makes small holes providing welcome ventilation. Goats' hair is therefore ideal, being waterproof, strong against the wind, and offering shade and ventilation from desert heat.

When a tent was erected, poles were pounded into the ground, and the goats' hair covering put over them. This covering was then secured with ropes attached to tent pegs also driven into the ground. There is a gruesome incident in the book of Judges, when 'Jael the wife of Heber took a tent peg, and took a hammer in her hand, and went softly to him

[Sisera, the commander of the Canaanite army] and drove the peg into his temple, till it went down into the ground, as he was lying fast asleep from weariness' (Judg. 4:21)—thus delivering Israel, albeit temporarily, from their enemies.

But what of the permanent spiritual lessons from 'dwelling in a tent'?

The fragility of life

Tent-dwelling reminds us of the fragility and impermanence of life in this world. One day, we will 'pull up the stakes' and leave this life for the next. Peter, in his last letter, referred to the human body as a tent. Knowing that his death was imminent, he wrote, 'I know that the putting off of my body [literally, 'tent'] will be soon' (2 Peter 1:14). Death is one of the few certainties of life: 'It is appointed for men to die once, and after that comes judgment' (Heb. 9:27). How vital it is, then, that we take into account the reality of death and 'Prepare to meet [our] God' (Amos 4:12). Scripture teaches that the only way we can face death with confidence is by knowing that our sins are forgiven—and the only way to know that our sins are forgiven is to trust in the Lord Jesus Christ. He died on Calvary's cross so that sinners who put their faith in Him might be saved from divine judgement. Scripture affirms, 'There is therefore now no condemnation for those who are in Christ Jesus' (Rom. 8:1).

Dependence on God

Tent-dwelling reminds us of our total dependence on God. One of the reasons why He instituted the 'Feast of Tents' was to remind the Israelites of His providence. They lived in tents in the wilderness for forty years. The wilderness is a dry, dead and barren place, but God's goodness sustained them. 'He … gave them bread from heaven in abundance. He opened the rock, and water gushed forth' (Ps. 105:40–41). Moses could say to them in truth, 'Your clothing did not wear out upon you, and your foot did not swell, these forty years' (Deut. 8:4). Life in the tent of this body of ours reminds us that we are not independent beings but dependent ones—totally dependent on God our Maker and Sustainer. 'In him we live and move and have our being' (Acts 17:28). God not only gives us life but also sustains our life.

The coming of Christ

Tent-dwelling points us to the central message of the Bible: that 'Christ Jesus came into the world to save sinners' (1 Tim. 1:15). John 1:14, speaking of the incarnation of Christ, says, 'the Word became flesh and dwelt among us, full of grace and truth.' A literal translation of this is, 'The Word became flesh and pitched His tent among us.'

Christ is God in a human body. In Christ God became man. In Christ the uncreated Creator stepped into His creation. 'In him the whole fulness of deity dwells bodily' (Col. 2:9). And why did God in Christ 'pitch His tent' here on earth? The Nicene Creed says it well: it was 'for us and for our salvation he came down from heaven … and was made man'.

'The wages of sin is death' (Rom. 6:23). Immortal deity cannot die. In His amazing grace, God became man so that He could die and so pay the wages of sin on our behalf. Christ took on human form so that He could die and procure our eternal salvation. Life in this earthly tent is both impermanent and uncertain. All its joys are undependable. The best that this world offers will come to an end. Contrast this with the 'solid joys and lasting treasures' which 'none but Zion's children know'.[1] As Paul wrote in 2 Corinthians 5:1, 'For we know that if the earthly tent we live in is destroyed, we have a building from God, a house not made with hands, eternal in the heavens.'

NOTE

1 John Newton, 'Glorious Things of Thee Are Spoken'.

Houses

Our basic human need for shelter unites us across the centuries with the people of Bible times. It is strange, considering our recent technological advances, that house-building has not changed very much since the days of the Bible. Houses are still built by cementing one brick on top of another, just as in early times when 'they had brick for stone, and bitumen for mortar' (Gen. 11:3).

At the time of the Lord Jesus, the majority of people's houses—as opposed to those of the rich or ruling minority—consisted of just one main living room. This living room had small, high windows. These did not let in much light, but kept the house warm in winter and pleasantly ventilated in summer. As the inside of the house was naturally quite dark, light was provided by small earthenware lamps. These could be both hand-held or put on a lamp stand. Whilst we tend to sleep in the dark, in Bible days there was a great fear of darkness, so people slept in the light. The 'virtuous wife' of Proverbs 31 therefore ensured that her house lamp had enough oil to keep its wick burning all night long: 'Her lamp does not go out at night' (Prov. 31:18).

The flat roofs which distinguished houses in Bible times can still be seen in the Middle East today. These flat roofs could be reached by an outside staircase. The roof was ideal for drying fruit and clothes, and would be slept on in summer time. Acts 10:9 significantly records that, one lunchtime, 'Peter went up on the housetop to pray'. It would seem that 'health and safety' was an issue even in Bible days, as it was stipulated in the law of Moses that the flat roof of a house had to have a small wall or parapet: 'When you build a new house, you shall make a parapet for your roof, that you may not bring the guilt of blood upon your house, if any one fall from it' (Deut. 22:8).

A house in Bible times was not very luxurious, but it was not really used much during the day. Adults worked and children played outside. At night, though, the family would all come in and they would be joined by their animals too—working animals such as sheep, goats and a mule, rather than pets. The family all slept together on mats which would be rolled up during the day.

Spiritual lessons

Houses contain many spiritual lessons. Before a house is built, a firm foundation must be dug and laid if the house is to stand up safe, sound and strong. And this is true in the spiritual realm too. On what are we building for eternity? What are our foundations? Can we say, 'On Christ the solid Rock I stand; all other ground is sinking sand'?[1] Jesus said,

Every one ... who hears these words of mine and does them will be like a wise man who built his house upon the rock; and the rain fell, and the floods came, and the winds blew and beat upon that house, but it did not fall, because it had been founded on the rock. And every one who hears these words of mine and does not do them will be like a foolish man who built his house upon the sand; and the rain fell, and the floods came, and the winds blew and beat against that house, and it fell; and great was the fall of it (Matt. 7:24–27).

A miracle in a house

Mark 2:1–12 describes a very crowded house with Jesus inside. Four anonymous men were anxious to bring their paralysed friend to the Saviour for healing. The crowd, though, prevented them. Undeterred, they carried their paralysed friend up the outside stairs to the roof, removed the roof tiles, dug an opening through the soft clay and lowered their mat-ridden friend to the feet of Jesus. Their effort was well rewarded. The first thing that Jesus said to the paralysed man was, 'My son, your sins are forgiven' (Mark 2:5). He dealt with the need of the soul before the need of the body. The need of the soul, however, is unseen. A forgiven soul does not show up under an X-ray! But Jesus next demonstrated that the forgiveness He bestows is real. He continued,

'But that you may know that the Son of man has authority on earth to forgive sins'—he said to the paralytic—'I say to you, rise, take up your pallet and go home.' And he rose, and immediately took up the pallet and went out before them all, so that they were all amazed and glorified God, saying, 'We never saw anything like this!' (Mark 2:10–12).

The paralysed man's transformation in that crowded house was evidence of the real spiritual transformation Jesus brought and still brings. 'Therefore, if any one is in Christ, he is a new creation; the old has passed away, behold, the new has come' (2 Cor. 5:17).

God answers prayer

A one-roomed house in the Bible also reminds us of the fact that our God hears and answers our prayers. Jesus once told a parable about a man who knocks urgently on his friend's house at midnight, seeking help. A guest has arrived. He needs to be fed, but the man's larder is empty. He therefore knocks and asks his friend, 'Friend, lend me three loaves' (Luke 11:5). His friend in the one-roomed house answers, 'Do not bother me; the door is now shut, and my children are with me in bed; I cannot get up and give you anything' (Luke 11:7). The man, though, persists, and the friend's reluctance and indolence are overcome. He gives the man what he needs for his visiting guest, thus alleviating his embarrassment.

Jesus told this parable to teach us that prayer to our Father in heaven is not a matter of overcoming God's reluctance, but rather of tapping into God's willingness. Jesus went on to say, 'Ask, and it will be given you; seek, and you will find; knock, and it will be opened to you. For every one who asks receives, and he who seeks finds, and to him who knocks it will be opened' (Luke 11:9–10).

The Father's house

Ordinarily, as we have said, houses in Bible times consisted of just one single room. Every Christian, by contrast, is destined to dwell in the most magnificent house—a dwelling greater than words can describe. Jesus said, 'In my Father's house are many rooms; if it were not so, would I have told you that I go to prepare a place for you?' (John 14:2).

Heaven, then, is 'God's house'. And God's house will be the eternal dwelling place of the believer. For the believer, heaven is home. Heaven is a prepared place for a prepared people. By His atoning death, Jesus has prepared us for heaven. And Scripture says that, if we belong to Jesus, He is currently preparing heaven for us. 'I go to prepare a place for you.' Truly, for the believer, the best is yet to be. 'No eye has seen, nor ear heard, nor the heart of man conceived, what God has prepared for those who love him' (1 Cor. 2:9).

NOTE

1   Edward Mote, 'My Hope Is Built on Nothing Less'.

Bread

Those who lived in Bible times would have looked at you blankly had you asked to borrow their mobile phone, check your email on their computer or for them to join you in watching the evening news on TV. Yet they, in common with us, also had to eat. Whatever the era or culture, food is essential to sustain life.

The people in Bible times—unlike us—used to eat only two meals a day. In the morning they had a light breakfast of bread, cheese and olives, often eaten after they had started work. Then in the evening, rather than having a meal on individual plates, a family would gather round a communal bowl of either meat or vegetable stew. Into this they would dip pieces of bread which they would then eat. The bread acted as a spoon—knives and forks were a long way off—and was perfectly hygienic, as no fingers touched the food. Bread was common to both meals. It was a staple of the daily diet. It is referred to in Leviticus 26:26 as 'your staff of bread'. Even today, bread is sometimes referred to as 'the staff of life'.

The traditional flat loaf of the Bible was made from ground wheat flour, or, if you were poorer, ground barley flour. The bread could be leavened or unleavened. Jesus once fed five thousand from the 'packed lunch' of 'a lad' who had 'five barley loaves and two fish' (John 6:9). Labour in Bible times was strictly demarcated by gender. Before the days of industrial-scale bakery, it was the responsibility of the women of the house to keep the home supplied with bread. 'A good wife ... provides food for her household' (Prov. 31:10, 15). This would have to be done every few days, as, before the discovery of our modern preservatives, bread soon went stale.

Bread-making

The bread-making process was as follows. First of all the women would manufacture flour by the manual grinding of grain between two millstones. Millstones were a common sight in Bible days. They were essential for the bread which sustains life. Thus Deuteronomy 24:6 reads, 'No man shall take a mill or an upper millstone in pledge; for he would be taking a life in pledge.' Judges 9:53 describes a millstone being used as an instrument of murder when 'a certain woman threw an upper millstone upon Abimelech's head [from the town wall] and crushed his skull'. Jesus said that when He comes again in power and great glory, 'There will be two women grinding together; one will be taken and the other left' (Luke 17:35).

Once the grain had been ground to make flour, water and salt was added to make a dough. Some fermented dough was added to this in the case of leavened bread. The dough was kneaded in a wooden bowl, and, in the case of leavened bread, left to rise. The dough was next shaped into flat loaves and baked in an oven.

Ovens in Bible times were neither gas nor electric! The simple oven was a bowl oven. A clay bowl was turned upside down over flat stones. The bread was baked on these flat stones. Underneath the stones the oven was fuelled by burning grass or even—distasteful as it sounds—animal dung. A variation on the bowl oven was the pit oven. This was basically a hole in the ground, into which the fuel was put, with the bake-stones placed on top. As time went on, however, public bakeries appeared. Women would then take their dough to a public oven to be baked. The baked bread would be delivered back to them by baker boys. One such public bakery was located in Jerusalem, for Jeremiah 37:21 relates how 'a loaf of bread was given him [Jeremiah] daily from the bakers' street'. Bread in Bible times, therefore, was both similar to and different from the wrapped, sliced variety with which we are familiar.

The Bread of Life
It is against the background of the centrality and necessity of bread in daily life that we understand Jesus' claim in John 6:35: 'I am the bread of life; he who comes to me shall not hunger, and he who believes in me shall never thirst.' Just as bread satisfies our physical hunger, so Jesus is able to satisfy our spiritual hunger. Just as bread is vital for life, so Jesus is indispensable if we are to know eternal life—that is, fellowship with God for time and eternity.

In John 6:51 Jesus explained further, 'I am the living bread which came down from heaven; if any one eats of this bread, he will live for ever; and the bread which I shall give for the life of the world is my flesh.' Jesus here is directing us to His death on the cross. Paradoxically, it is by the death of Christ on the cross that we come to have eternal life, for it is through the death of Christ on the cross for our sins that we enjoy the forgiveness of our sins and reconciliation to God the Father now and for ever. On the cross, Jesus' words were fulfilled. The bread which He gave for the life of the world was His own flesh. He gave Himself as an atoning sacrifice. We take and eat physical bread and our hunger is satisfied. We take and eat the 'Bread of Life'—that is, we put our faith in Christ as our own personal Saviour—and we are eternally saved and spiritually satisfied. Four hours or so after a meal, we are hungry again. Once we trust in Christ, however, we are never spiritually hungry again. He saves, keeps and satisfies. The one who comes to Jesus shall never hunger!

Sacramental bread
Bread is essential for life. Jesus and His death on the cross are indispensable for eternal life. Interestingly, bread features in a commandment which Jesus gave to ensure that we always keep His atoning death in mind. He ordained the Lord's Supper as a perpetual memorial of His saving death: 'the Lord Jesus on the night when he was betrayed took bread, and when he had given thanks, he broke it, and

said, "This is my body which is for you. Do this in remembrance of me"'
(1 Cor. 11:23–24).

The Lord's Supper entails the breaking and eating of bread, and the
pouring out and drinking of wine, in commemoration of how Jesus'
sinless body was broken and His precious blood poured out on Calvary
for the sinner's salvation. The Lord's Supper is multifaceted. One facet is
a reminder that Jesus is the Bread of Life. John Calvin explains:

This is why the body and blood are represented to us by means of bread and wine, so
that we learn not only that they are ours, but that they are life and nourishment to us.
Thus when we see the bread consecrated as the body of Christ, at that moment we
should see this parallel in our minds: as bread feeds and preserves the life of the body,
so the body of Christ is the nourishment and protection of our spiritual life.[1]

Now none but Christ can satisfy,
None other name for me;
There's love and life and lasting joy,
Lord Jesus, found in Thee.[2]

Thou art the bread of life, O Lord, to me,
Thy holy Word the truth that saveth me;
Give me to eat and live with Thee above;
Teach me to love the truth, for Thou art love.[3]

NOTES

1   John Calvin, *Truth for All Time* (Edinburgh: Banner of Truth, 1998), p. 67.
2   Frances Bevan, 'O Christ, in Thee My Soul Hath Found'.
3   Mary Lathbury/Alexander Groves, 'Break Thou the Bread of Life'.

Clothing

Did you know that the first ever human clothes were actually made and provided by God Himself? Genesis 3:21 tells us that 'the LORD God made for Adam and for his wife garments of skins, and clothed them'. Here, at the dawn of history, when sin had entered the world, God graciously covered our ancestors' shame. It is a picture of salvation. The Hebrew word 'to atone' can also mean 'to cover'. God graciously provided an atonement—a covering—for sin. The provision, though, entailed the death of an animal. So here, then, at the dawn of time, we have a pointer to the Lord Jesus Christ: for our sin to be atoned for, and our guilt and shame to be covered in the sight of God, the sinless Saviour had to die.

The clothes of Christ

References to Christ's clothing in the Bible are somewhat sparse. John records that, at the 'last supper' in the upper room, Christ 'rose from supper, laid aside his garments, and girded himself with a towel. Then he poured water into a basin, and began to wash the disciples' feet, and to wipe them with the towel with which he was girded' (John 13:4–5). Here Christ was taking upon Himself the role of a menial household slave whose job it was to wash the feet of guests. The act is remarkable considering His divine status. This event, although historical, also seems to be parabolic of Christ's ministry as a whole. Jesus Himself said, 'the Son of man … came not to be served but to serve, and to give his life as a ransom for many' (Mark 10:45). An early Christian creedal-hymn stated, 'though he was in the form of God [he] did not count equality with God a thing to be grasped, but emptied himself, taking the form of a servant' (Phil. 2:6–7).

The Gospels contain accounts of an anonymous sick woman who was healed by touching the garment Christ wore. Matthew's account records, 'behold, a woman who had suffered from a hemorrhage for twelve years came up behind him and touched the fringe of his garment' (Matt. 9:20). Jesus commended her for her faith, and Matthew records, 'And instantly the woman was made well' (Matt. 9:22). The 'fringe' or 'tassel' in question here was worn by Christ in obedience to the law of Moses, which stated, 'You shall make yourself tassels on the four corners of your cloak' (Deut. 22:12). Numbers 15 is more detailed in its explanation. Here, the LORD commanded Moses, 'Speak to the people of Israel, and bid them to make tassels on the corners of their garments throughout their generations, and to put upon the tassel of each corner a cord of blue; and it shall be to you a tassel to look upon and remember all the commandments of the LORD' (vv. 37–39). The tassel, then, was a kind of 'visual aid'. 'Blue' speaks of heaven above, the dwelling place of God. The tassel was made up of eight threads—a reminder of God's covenant with Abraham which commanded males to be circumcised on the eighth day. It also had five knots—a reminder of the five books of Moses, the sacred Torah.

The healing of the woman with the haemorrhage was not so much brought about by the tassel of Christ but by the Christ who wore the tassel. Jesus commended her for her faith in Him, saying, 'Take heart, daughter; your faith has made you well' (Matt. 9:22). Faith is still the human channel by which we receive the blessing of Christ. The woman's healing is a picture of Christian salvation:

She only touched the hem of His garment
As to His side she stole,
Amid the crowd that gathered around Him,
And straightway she was whole.

Oh, touch the hem of His garment!
And thou, too, shalt be free!
His saving power this very hour
Shall give new life to thee![1]

Christ's seamless robe

Psalm 22 gives us the most remarkable and vivid description of the cross of Calvary, although it was written around 1000 BC. Among the many prophecies it makes is a reference to the clothing of the coming crucified Christ. Psalm 22:18 reads, 'they divide my garments among them, and for my raiment they cast lots.' The prophecy was fulfilled down to the letter, in the fullness of time. John relates,

When the soldiers had crucified Jesus they took his garments and made four parts, one for each soldier; also his tunic [that is, His undergarment]. But the tunic was without seam, woven from top to bottom; so they said to one another, 'Let us not tear it, but cast lots for it to see whose it shall be.' This was to fulfil the scripture,

'They parted my garments among them,
and for my clothing they cast lots' (John 19:23–24).

Christ's crucifixion was supervised by four Roman soldiers. Taking the personal belongings of a crucified victim was seen as a 'perk of the job'. They divided Christ's clothing among them. One had the turban—the head-covering which He would have worn. One had his footwear—a pair of sandals. One had his outer garment, and another had his leather belt, or girdle. This left one garment over: His seamless tunic. A seamless tunic was valuable. It would have been a shame to ruin it by cutting it up into four parts, so the soldiers decided they would gamble for it. The winner of the dice got the robe. In gambling for Christ's robe as they did, unbeknown to them, they fulfilled the Scriptures of God.

Christ's seamless robe has often been viewed as depicting His sinless life. At Calvary, however, He gave His sinless life in sacrifice, to atone for sinners. At Calvary, a great transaction occurred. Christ's seamless robe was taken off Him, and our sins were laid upon Him. All this was so that we could be saved—clothed with His righteousness, and so made fit for God's presence. 'For our sake he made him to be sin who knew no sin, so that in him we might become the righteousness of God' (2 Cor. 5:21).

Salvation entails a change of clothes! Salvation is a discarding of the filthy garments of sin and a putting-on of the perfect righteousness of Christ, freely given at Calvary. Such is the joy known by Christians alone: 'I will greatly rejoice in the LORD, my soul shall exult in my God; for he has clothed me with the garments of salvation, he has covered me with the robe of righteousness' (Isa. 61:10).

Jesus, Thy blood and righteousness
My beauty are, my glorious dress;
'Midst flaming worlds, in these arrayed,
With joy shall I lift up my head.

This spotless robe the same appears,
When ruined nature sinks in years;
No age can change its glorious hue,
The robe of Christ is ever new.[2]

NOTES

1   George F. Root, 'She Only Touched the Hem of His Garment'.
2   Nikolaus L. von Zinzendorf, 'Jesus, Thy Blood and Righteousness'.

Marriage

Although the people of Bible times lived in a very different cultural setting from ours, in common with us they used to get married. Proverbs 18:22 reads, 'He who finds a wife finds a good thing, and obtains favor from the LORD.' The Bible teaches that monogamous heterosexual marriage is a divine ordinance originating at the dawn of human history. Genesis 2:24 tells us, 'Therefore a man leaves his father and his mother and cleaves to his wife, and they become one flesh.'

Interestingly, the very first miracle which the Lord Jesus performed—the turning of water into wine—occurred at a wedding feast: 'On the third day there was a marriage at Cana in Galilee … Jesus also was invited to the marriage, with his disciples' (John 2:1–2). Jewish weddings were always held on 'the third day' after the Sabbath—our Tuesday. On the third day of creation, 'The earth brought forth vegetation, plants yielding seed according to their own kinds, and trees bearing fruit in which is their seed, each according to its kind. And God saw that it was good' (Gen. 1:12). Jewish weddings were held on 'the third day' with the hope that the marriage would be similarly fruitful and good.

The age at which a person was eligible to marry was different in Bible times from today. Girls then were betrothed when they were as young as twelve to seventeen years of age. Their husbands could be a little or a lot older. Unlike our Western 'romantic' weddings, the process of getting married in Bible times involved three distinct stages:

The choice of a bride

First of all, the prospective groom's parents would choose a wife for their son. Marriages in Bible days were arranged marriages—the bride and groom had little or no say in the matter. Whereas in the West we tend to fall in love and then get married, in Bible days it was more a case of getting married and then falling in love. The groom's parents would negotiate for a suitable wife with the potential bride's parents.

Purchasing a bride

Secondly, a sum of money—a dowry—was paid to the bride's parents by the groom's parents. This compensated them for the lack of their daughter's services in the future when she moved out of her parental home. Fifty shekels was the normal price for a wife, but goods or services could be negotiated instead. When the dowry was paid, the bride and groom met up for the first time. A binding legal betrothal was then made in writing, and the couple pledged themselves to each other. This gives us some insight into Joseph's horror when he found that Mary, his wife-to-be, was expecting a child. Joseph and Mary were not yet married, but only pledged to be married. Initially, Joseph feared that Mary had been unfaithful, so he sought to cancel the wedding and annul the betrothal. It took angelic assurance to convince Joseph that Mary's pregnancy was a result of the working of the Spirit of God and that she was therefore still a virgin.

Marrying the bride

About a year after the dowry was paid and the pledges were made, the actual wedding would take place. The year gave the groom time to organize a house and home. With great ceremony and celebration, the groom and his friends would go in procession to the bride's house, collect her and take her to his house. Music and dancing accompanied the procession. Once in the groom's house, blessings would be said and then feasting and partying would begin. Our Western wedding receptions tend to last for an afternoon and perhaps an evening. Wedding feasts in Bible times, however, could last for many days. Once the feast was over, however, the bride and groom would settle down together, and the ups and downs of everyday living would begin.

Christ has a bride

Did you know that the three stages of a wedding in Bible times illustrate what it is to be a Christian? They depict Christian salvation. The New Testament depicts the church—the community of the redeemed—as 'the bride of Christ'. He is pledged to her in covenant love, and she reciprocates this in covenant love and loyalty. Consider the three stages once again:

Firstly, *marriages were arranged: a bride was chosen*. The Christian also has been chosen. The Bible teaches that the ultimate origin of our salvation is not our choice of Christ in time, but God's choice of us, in Christ, in eternity past. 'He chose us in him before the foundation of the world' (Eph. 1:4).

Secondly, *a wife was purchased*. The Christian also has been purchased. We have been redeemed. 'To redeem' means 'to set free by the paying of a price'. The price of our redemption from the penalty and power of sin was Christ's own precious blood. 'In him we have redemption through his blood, the forgiveness of our trespasses according to the riches of his grace' (Eph. 1:7). A hymn concerning the church contains the lines:

From heaven He came and sought her
To be His holy bride;
With His own blood He bought her
And for her life He died.[1]

Thirdly, *in due time, the groom took his bride to his house and the wedding festivities began*. And it is similar with Christian salvation. The Bible looks forward to the time when the Christian's present salvation will be consummated—enjoyed in a much fuller and richer way. It depicts this as an eternal wedding feast with Christ, in His home. 'Blessed are those who are invited to the marriage supper of the Lamb' (Rev. 19:9). The Christian's future is thus brighter than bright. Our current lot may involve unhappiness. Our eternal lot is promised to be happy—feasting with Christ our Saviour.

Wedding wear

Finally, we note that at wedding feasts in Bible times, all guests were given a wedding garment to wear. This made everyone from every background—whether wealthy or poor—equal. Jesus once told a parable about a man who was thrown out of a wedding feast as he was not wearing the required wedding garment. The king who gave the feast said to him, 'Friend, how did you get in here without a wedding garment?' (Matt. 22:11).

Aware of our sin, we are rightly aware of our unfitness to feast in God's house and enjoy His presence. He is infinitely righteous, whereas we are all unrighteous. But the Good News of the gospel is that the righteousness which God demands and the righteousness which we require is a righteousness freely bestowed on us in Christ. On the cross, Christ took our sin away. And because of the cross, the perfect righteousness of Christ is imputed to the believer. 'For our sake he made him to be sin who knew no sin, so that in him we might become the righteousness of God' (2 Cor. 5:21). We will thus enjoy the heavenly feast, not because of our merit, but because of God's mercy. Salvation is gained not by our own righteousness, but by the righteousness of Christ. Here is a cause to celebrate—eternally!

I will greatly rejoice in the LORD,
  my soul shall exult in my God;
for he has clothed me with the garments of salvation,
  he has covered me with the robe of righteousness,
as a bridegroom decks himself with a garland,
  and as a bride adorns herself with her jewels (Isa. 61:10).

NOTE

1   Samuel John Stone, 'The Church's One Foundation'.

Death and burial

The people who lived in Bible times had to cope with the sad experience of death, loss and bereavement just as we do. Death and grief are no respecters of the centuries. The people of the Bible died, just as all of us will eventually die, due to illness, old age, accident or murder.

At the dawn of history, God pronounced to Adam and all his descendants, 'You are dust, and to dust you shall return' (Gen. 3:19). Death, according to the Bible, has more than one facet to it. It can refer to the separation of the soul from the body—physical death—but also to the separation of the soul from God—spiritual death. The Bible teaches that death is God's judgement on sin: 'The wages of sin is death' (Rom. 6:23). It is against this dark background that the Christian gospel really shines. Jesus came to give us life—eternal life. Eternal life refers to unblemished fellowship with God our Maker: 'The wages of sin is death, but the free gift of God is eternal life in Christ Jesus our Lord' (Rom. 6:23).

Burial customs

In Bible times, burial took place within twenty-four hours of a person's death. The hotter climate made a body decompose quickly. The immediate family would then mourn for seven days, 'sitting *shiva*' on low stools—the word *shiva* is derived from the Hebrew word for 'week' or 'seven'.

The dead person's body would be washed and wrapped in bandages mingled with aromatic spices. The head and the body were bound separately. The corpse would then be carried in procession in an open coffin—or bier—to the grave, often accompanied by 'professional mourners'. If the family were poor or of ordinary means, the body would be buried in a shallow grave with a slab of stone on the top. This stone was painted white, to warn people of the danger of the ritual uncleanness resulting from touching it. The law of Moses stated, 'He who touches the dead body of any person shall be unclean seven days' (Num. 19:11). By extension, this also applied to tombstones. All this underlies Jesus' words in Mathew 23:27: 'Woe to you, scribes and Pharisees, hypocrites! for you are like whitewashed tombs, which outwardly appear beautiful, but within they are full of dead men's bones and all uncleanness.'

People of richer means were buried in caves or tombs carved out of a rock. These had shelving on which the body was laid. A large boulder was placed at the grave's entrance to deter wild animals and grave-robbers. Although the Lord Jesus and His earthly family were not financially rich, the Lord Jesus received a rich man's burial. Scripture prophesied, 'they made his grave with the wicked and with a rich man in his death' (Isa. 53:9). The Scripture was fulfilled when 'a rich man from Arimathea named Joseph … asked for the body of Jesus … wrapped it in a clean linen shroud, and laid it in his own new tomb, which he had hewn in the rock' (Matt. 27:57–60).

The defeat of death

The morbid subject of death and burial reminds us that we still live in a fallen, imperfect world. Death is a fact of life. At the heart of the Christian faith, however, lies an empty tomb, for at the heart of the Christian faith lies the resurrection of Christ. Jesus overcame death and conquered the grave. And the Bible promises that all who are united to Him by faith will most surely do likewise.

John's account of Christ's resurrection is a vivid eyewitness one. We mentioned above that the body and head of a corpse were bound separately. John relates how Peter went into Jesus' tomb on the first Easter Sunday and 'saw the linen cloths lying, and the napkin, which had been on his head, not lying with the linen cloths but rolled up in a place by itself' (John 20:6–7). Miraculously, Jesus had passed through His grave-clothes, leaving them undisturbed. He was later seen, heard and touched by many. The evidence for Christ's resurrection is broadly twofold: (1) His grave was empty; (2) the risen Christ appeared.

Christ's resurrection has many consequences and blessed implications. It proves first of all that He is the very Son of God—'designated Son of God in power according to the Spirit of holiness by his resurrection from the dead' (Rom. 1:4). Christ's resurrection is also God the Father's endorsement of the sacrifice His Son offered for sinners on Calvary's cross: He 'was put to death for our trespasses and raised for our justification' (Rom. 4:25). And Christ's resurrection is the pledge that all who belong to Him will one day be resurrected—we will rise to a fuller, richer, more glorious life, able to glorify God and enjoy Him in a way we have never known before. 'Christ has been raised from the dead, the first fruits of those who have fallen asleep. For as by a man came death, by a man has come also the resurrection of the dead' (1 Cor. 15:20–21).

Death is sad and seems so final. We grieve the loss of our loved ones still. For the Christian, however, death is not the end, but rather the beginning. 'The sting of death is sin' (1 Cor. 15:56). In dying for our sins, Jesus has taken away the sting of death. For believers, death is the porter which ushers us into the nearer presence of our Saviour. We can thus say, 'For to me to live is Christ, and to die is gain' (Phil. 1:21). The ultimate Christian hope—that is, our confident expectation based on the promises of God in Christ—is not the salvation of the soul but the resurrection of the body. On a coming day, the Bible says, 'the Lord Jesus Christ … will change our lowly body to be like his glorious body, by the power which enables him even to subject all things to himself' (Phil. 3:21).

Ploughing, sowing and reaping

B read—made of either wheat or barley—was a staple of the diet in Bible times. The production of bread depended on a good supply of grain, and grain was produced by farming. Agriculture was as integral to the economy of Israel in Bible times as it is for us today.

In Deuteronomy 11:14 we read that 'he [the LORD) will give the rain for your land in its season, the early rain and the later rain, that you may gather in your grain'. The 'early rain' here refers to the autumn rain, and the 'later rain' refers to the spring rain. Both were essential for grain to be grown. Ploughing was undertaken in the autumn when the early rain had softened the ground. The seed was scattered or 'broadcast' into the furrows made. Winter then came, and the ground hardened and could not be worked. The later rain of spring, though, softened the ground again. This, along with the early sunshine, swelled the grain and made the stalks grow. In the later spring-time the crop was ready to be harvested. The stalks were cut by hand with a sickle or scythe and taken to a hard threshing floor, where they were threshed using a heavy sledge. What remained was then 'winnowed'—that is, tossed into the air with a winnowing fork. This separated the chaff from the grain. The wind carried the chaff away to one side, whilst the grain was gathered into a heap. The grain was then taken to the market to be sold. Before it could be ground for bread-making, though, it had to be finally sieved, lest either stones or 'darnel' had got amongst the grain. Darnel was a type of grass which was believed to be poisonous.

Eastern agricultural implements contain many instructive spiritual lessons for us.

The yoke

The yoke used for ploughing was a beam of wood put onto two oxen, enabling them to draw an iron plough and so dig the soil while guided and 'goaded' by the farmer. Jesus once said, 'Take my yoke upon you, and learn from me … For my yoke is easy, and my burden is light' (Matt. 11:29). This reminds us that we have to work for Jesus out of gratitude for our salvation, and that the work we do for Him will be fruitful and wonderfully fulfilling. His yoke fits comfortably and rides easily.

For two oxen to pull a plough together comfortably, they had to be of a compatible size. This would not be the case if an ox and an ass were yoked together; hence the law stated, 'You shall not plow with an ox and an ass together' (Deut. 22:10). Paul takes up this imagery in 2 Corinthians 6:14, where he forbids a believer marrying an unbeliever. Such would be a painful mismatch. It would be an unequal yoke—incompatible on a spiritual level.

The goad

This was an iron spike held by the farmer as he ploughed. He would use it to clean his plough so that it would furrow effectively. He would also use it to train his oxen. Initially they might rebel against having a yoke on them, and try to kick to free themselves from it. The farmer, though, held a goad. Kicking this spike hurt. The oxen soon stopped and ploughed on in a straight line.

On the Damascus road, the risen Christ said to Saul of Tarsus as he persecuted the church, 'Saul, Saul, why do you persecute me? It hurts you to kick against *the goads*' (Acts 26:14).[1] From that moment Saul—better known as Paul—stopped his rebellion and submitted to the Lord's will and way. He was to become one of the greatest Christian ambassadors and exponents ever.

The handle

A plough had only one handle. This was guided by the farmer with one hand, whilst with his other hand he held the goad. To plough in a straight line, the plougher had to look at a fixed point ahead and not be distracted. He also had to look out for any stones or rocks which might damage the plough. Jesus made a spiritual application from this when He said, 'No one who puts his hand to the plow and looks back is fit for the kingdom of God' (Luke 9:62). We are to keep our eyes on the Saviour and beware of anything which might impede or distract from our fellowship with Him.

The tribulum

This was the name given to the threshing sledge on which the farmer sat to give it weight. It was pulled by an animal over the stalks of grain to separate them in preparation for winnowing. From this 'tribulum' we get the word 'tribulation'. In the providence of God, every Christian is sure to go through tribulation. Paul exhorts us to 'be patient in tribulation' (Rom. 12:12). God is always kind and purposeful in His dealings with His children. He uses tribulation to draw us closer to Himself. Tribulation—when sanctified to us—produces in us the purer grain of total trust and dependence on God and cuts away anything which hinders this.

A gospel application

The New Testament abounds in ploughing and reaping metaphors. James, for instance, commands us to 'receive with meekness the implanted word, which is able to save your souls' (James 1:21). He surely had Jesus' famous 'Parable of the Sower'—or perhaps more correctly 'The Parable of the Soils'—in mind here.

Jesus likened the sowing of seed to the preaching of the gospel—see Mark 4:1–20. When the gospel is preached, people react in different ways. Some have the Word taken away by Satan—just as some seed in a field falls on a path and is eaten by birds. Some believe for a while and then fall away—just as some seed grows at the start, but does not take deep root. Some people seem to believe for a while, but then get distracted, and the gospel does not come to full fruition in them—just like seed which ends up choked by being sown among thorns. Some, however, hear the Good News of Jesus, put their faith in Him and are surely saved, bearing fruit to eternal life—just like the seed sown in the field that 'fell into good soil and brought forth grain, growing up and increasing and yielding thirtyfold, and sixtyfold and a hundredfold (Mark 4:8). The 'Parable of the Soils' makes us search our hearts. It makes us ask ourselves, 'Am I a true believer? What kind of soil is the soil of my heart? Has the gospel taken root, and is it bearing fruit in me?'

Preaching the gospel is like sowing seed. The hearts and ears of those who hear it are like different kinds of soil. The Word of God, however, is sure to accomplish God's work. God has said, 'my word … that goes forth from my mouth … shall not return to me empty, but it shall accomplish that which I purpose, and prosper in the thing for which I sent it' (Isa. 55:11). He has His elect and He will surely save them in His time, through the preaching of the gospel. Preachers, therefore, are to take courage and, by God's grace, 'plough on'. 'He that goes forth weeping, bearing the seed for sowing, shall come home with shouts of joy, bringing his sheaves with him' (Ps. 126:6).

The final harvest

In Bible days it was known that wheat and weeds grew together. As they grew, they were indistinguishable. It was only at harvest time that their true nature was revealed, and they were separated accordingly. This practice was evidently known to the Lord Jesus, for in a parable Jesus stated, 'Let both grow together until the harvest; and at harvest time I will tell the reapers, "Gather the weeds first and bind them in bundles to be burned, but gather the wheat into my barn"' (Matt. 13:30).

Jesus used this practice as a formidable illustration of what will happen at the end of the world—at the final harvest: 'Just as the weeds are gathered and burned with fire, so will it be at the close of the age' (Matt. 13:40). The Lord Jesus Christ is thus the great Divider of humanity as well as the great Reconciler of humanity. He divides us all into wheat and weeds—the saved and the unsaved, believers and unbelievers, those destined for 'God's barn' and those destined for the eternal flames.

It is stark, but the Bible is clear. Our attitude to Jesus determines where we will spend eternity—in heaven or in hell. 'He who believes in the Son has eternal life; he who does not obey the Son shall not see life, but the wrath of God rests upon him' (John 3:36). Or, as John the Baptist said of Christ, 'He will … gather his wheat into the granary, but the chaff he will burn with unquenchable fire' (Matt. 3:12).

NOTE

1   All emphasis in italics in Scripture quotes is mine.

The olive tree

The olive tree is symbolic of the land of the Bible. The 'Promised Land' is described in Deuteronomy 8:8 as 'a land of wheat and barley, of vines and fig trees and pomegranates, a land of *olive trees* and honey'.

The olive harvest was integral to the economy in Bible times. At a basic level, the olives provided both food and light. Olives were a staple of the diet, and olive oil was the normal fuel for lamps. Olive oil was also used medicinally, being employed as a soothing lotion for the skin. And olive oil was used in religious ceremonies: prophets, priests and kings were all anointed with oil at the outset of their ministries. Oil was symbolic of the Holy Spirit. The ceremonial anointing with oil symbolized being set apart by God for a specific ministry and being equipped with God's Holy Spirit to fulfil that ministry. Interestingly, the word 'Christ' is not a name but a title. It means 'the anointed one'. The Bible records the Lord Jesus being especially anointed with the Holy Spirit at the outset of His ministry. At His baptism 'the heaven was opened, and the Holy Spirit descended upon him in bodily form, as a dove' (Luke 3:21–22). As *the* Christ or Messiah, the Lord Jesus combines the threefold roles of prophet, priest and king in His one person.

Gethsemane: the Mount of Olives

On the east of Jerusalem stands the Mount of Olives. During the time of Christ, this mount was covered with olive groves. On the Mount of Olives, even today, the 'Garden of Gethsemane' can be visited. The name 'Gethsemane' means 'olive press'. The olive press was used to extract olive oil from olives. It was in Gethsemane's garden that the Lord Jesus prayed before going to the cross of Calvary. As He contemplated the cross and what it meant to be 'made … sin' (2 Cor. 5:21) He was 'greatly distressed and troubled' (Mark 14:33)—'pressed in', we could say. Yet He submitted to the will of God, saying, 'Not what I will, but what thou wilt' (Mark 14:36), and the cost notwithstanding, went ahead to fulfil God's plan of redemption, being 'obedient unto death, even death on a cross' (Phil. 2:8).

The olive harvest

Olives were harvested in the autumn. The average tree contained some ten to fifteen gallons of oil when processed. The fruit was gathered by climbing the tree and shaking it or beating it with rods. The law mercifully stipulated, 'When you beat your olive trees, you shall not go over the boughs again; it shall be for the sojourner, the fatherless, and the widow' (Deut. 24:20). The olives which fell on the ground were put into a circular stone olive press. An animal was then tethered to a large millstone put into the olive press, and made to walk blindfold in circles. As the animal did so, the olives were crushed and the oil ran out through channels and was collected in vats. This was considered to be the best olive oil. The remaining pulp in the olive mill, though, was not discarded. It was put into a wooden olive press and crushed further, extracting the very last drop of oil. This oil was not of the finest quality, but was perfectly useable for lighting the characteristic clay oil lamps of Bible times. Olives thus provided food, light and medicine. The process to obtain this, though, involved beating, bruising and crushing. And here we have a picture which gives us insight into the death of Jesus and the blessing of salvation which ensued:

The picture of the olive tree

First of all, we note that the olive tree was beaten. At His mock trial, the Lord Jesus was also beaten. The soldiers of the Roman governor mocked Him with a scarlet robe, a crown of thorns and a reed for a royal sceptre.

Matthew records that 'they spat upon him, and took the reed and struck him on the head' (Matt. 27:30).

The olives which fell from the beating were next put into the olive press for crushing. Likewise, after His beating, the Lord Jesus was crucified. Here He was really put into the 'olive press'. He was crushed by the load of human sin which was transferred to Him. And He was crushed by the fearsome wrath of God upon that load of sin. Just as olives were crushed and bruised to achieve the desired result, likewise the Lord Jesus 'was wounded for our transgressions, he was bruised for our iniquities; upon him was the chastisement that made us whole, and with his stripes we are healed' (Isa. 53:5).

The bruising and crushing of olives, however, was not pointless but purposeful. A good, pleasant and wholesome effect resulted. Olives brought vital food, light and healing.

Similarly, Jesus is our spiritual food. He said, 'I am the bread of life; he who comes to me shall not hunger, and he who believes in me shall never thirst' (John 6:35).

Jesus is also our light. He said, 'I am the light of the world; he who follows me will not walk in darkness, but will have the light of life' (John 8:12).

Jesus is our healing. He said, 'Those who are well have no need of a physician, but those who are sick; I came not to call the righteous, but sinners' (Mark 2:17). Sin is a sick state. Our sin alienates us from God our Maker. Through Christ's death on the cross for our sins, however, our relationship with God is healed and our fellowship with Him restored.

The olive tree was central to the economy in Bible times. And it is the Lord Jesus who is central to the Christian life, and the tree of Calvary that is indispensable for our eternal salvation. Christians are a saved people, and Christians will yet be a saved people. The Bible holds out the thrilling prospect of living in redeemed bodies on a redeemed earth for all who belong to Jesus. For the believer, the best is yet to be. The olive tree in full bloom is a beautiful sight to behold. Through Hosea the prophet, God used this familiar sight to depict the future glory of God's people. He said, 'I will be as the dew to Israel; he shall blossom as the lily, he shall strike root as the poplar; his shoots shall spread out; his beauty shall be *like the olive*, and his fragrance like Lebanon' (Hosea 14:5–6).

Pottery

It is highly likely that the day you read this you have used some form of pottery—a mug, cup, saucer or plate. Pottery unites us with those who lived in Bible times, for pottery is almost as old as civilization. In Bible times every village would have its potter. He would make such everyday items as clay oil lamps, pitchers for getting water from the village well, cooking pots and vessels for storing food, olive oil and wine.

The craft

A potter would set about his work as follows. First of all, he would obtain some clay from a river bank. Having dug this up, he would leave it in the sun for a day or two. Next, he would clean it of any foreign objects, picking out any twigs or stones. Then he would add a little water and knead it, until it became smooth and malleable. He would either use this clay as it was, or he would add a little crushed limestone to it.

A potter would sit at a potter's wheel. On this he would mould and shape the clay into the desired vessel. The wheel had both an upper and a lower circular surface. On the upper surface the potter would shape the clay with his hands. The lower wheel was linked to the upper one by a shaft. This enabled the upper wheel to be spun when the potter manipulated the lower wheel with his foot. Once the vessel had been shaped, it would be left to harden, either in the sunshine or by being baked in an oven. Once finished, it would be taken to the marketplace to be sold.

But are there any spiritual lessons to be gleaned from a potter at the wheel? Yes, there are:

The divine Potter

In Isaiah 64:8, the prophet confesses to God, 'O LORD, thou art our Father; we are the clay, and thou art our potter; we are all the work of thy hand.' This reminds us of Genesis 2:7, where we read how, at the dawn of history, 'the LORD God formed man of dust from the ground, and breathed into his nostrils the breath of life; and man became a living being.'

We must remember our place: we are clay! Almighty God is our Maker—He is our heavenly Potter. As such, He has the right of ownership to do with us just as He sees fit. Ultimately, our eternal destiny—heaven or hell—rests on His decision: what in eternity past He decided to do with us. His will is the will that will be done. Does this seem harsh to you? There were some who thought so in Paul's day. But consider Paul's response to this:

You will say to me then, 'Why does he still find fault? For who can resist his will?' But who are you, a man, to answer back to God? Will what is molded say to its molder, 'Why have you made me thus?' Has the potter no right over the clay, to make out of the same lump one vessel for beauty and another for menial use? What if God, desiring to show his wrath and to make known his power, has endured with much patience the vessels of wrath made for destruction, in order to make known the riches of his glory for the vessels of mercy, which he has prepared beforehand for glory …? (Rom. 9:19–23).

Paul is saying, in effect, 'Let God be God.' He is the Potter; we are the clay. He has the absolute right to make us either a vessel of mercy, destined for glory, or a vessel of wrath, destined for destruction.

Human frailty

Secondly, pottery reminds us of the frailty of our current bodies—these human bodies in which we experience the joy of salvation. In 2 Corinthians

4:7 Paul explains how 'we have this treasure [the treasure of salvation] in earthen vessels'. Ecclesiastes 12:6 reads, 'the pitcher is broken at the fountain.' Unglazed pottery in Bible days was notoriously brittle and easily broken. If a pitcher was put down too hastily on the rim of a well, the vessel might break and the water be lost.

The 'earthen vessels' in which we experience the salvation of God in Christ are also somewhat fragile. We are all subject to illness, weakness, old age and deterioration. We all live through times of physical and mental pain. Unlike the water in a pitcher, though, our salvation can never be lost. Our salvation, however, although real, is not yet complete. 'The redemption of our bodies' (Rom. 8:23) lies in the future. With our human frailties in mind, perhaps we should be more careful how we treat each other. If we knew another person's full situation, perhaps we would see a 'FRAGILE: HANDLE WITH CARE' notice on him or her. This, though, should not detract from our future Christian hope: 'the sufferings of this present time are not worth comparing with the glory that is to be revealed to us' (Rom. 8:18).

The Potter's ongoing work

Finally, pottery teaches us to take heart. If Almighty God really is our heavenly Potter, and if we belong to Jesus, He has not finished with us yet. He will surely shape us into the people He would have us be, to His glory. In Jeremiah 18 the prophet relates God's word to him:

'Arise, and go down to the potter's house, and there I will let you hear my words.' So I went down to the potter's house, and there he was working at his wheel. And the vessel he was making of clay was spoiled in the potter's hand, and he reworked it into another vessel, as it seemed good to the potter to do.

Then the word of the LORD came to me: 'O house of Israel, can I not do with you as this potter has done? says the LORD. Behold, like the clay in the potter's hand, so are you in my hand, O house of Israel.'

We are sinners saved by grace. The best Christian on earth has his or her character flaws and imperfections. But God has not finished with us yet! We are in His workshop, but destined for His showroom. There we will be flawless! There we will be conformed to the image of Christ, to the eternal glory of God. The Bible tells us so. 'I am sure that he who began a good work in you will bring it to completion at the day of Jesus Christ' (Phil. 1:6).

The carpenter

'**I**s not this the *carpenter's* son?' they asked of Jesus in Matthew 13:55. Similarly, in Mark 6:3 they asked, 'Is not this the *carpenter*, the son of Mary?' The true answer to these questions is actually 'Yes and no.' Yes, because the Lord Jesus was indeed a carpenter until He reached thirty years of age, whereupon He became a full-time itinerant preacher, teacher and healer. To describe Him as 'the carpenter's son' is true to the era of the first century, for in those days it was normal practice for a father to pass on his trade to his son. After an elementary education, a son would become his father's apprentice. Jesus thus followed Joseph, His legal father, and was what the Greek New Testament terms a *tekton*: a worker in wood and stone—a carpenter.

Carpenters

Carpenters in Bible days earned their living through manual work, by making necessary everyday objects such as roofs for houses, shutters for windows and the furniture for inside a house—tables, chairs and boxes for storage. The wood used would have been either hard olive wood and oak, or soft Jerusalem sycamore. When Solomon built the temple along with his own palace, however, expensive cedar wood from Lebanon was imported. In those days, the trees producing the wood were felled by hand, which entailed hard labour.

Had we been able to glimpse the Lord Jesus at work in His carpenter's workshop, we would have noticed the everyday tools of His trade—a saw to cut wood to a precise size; a stone-headed hammer to drive in nails; a wood plane to smooth and shape; a ruler and compass to measure; and a primitive drill to drill holes into wood. All these tools depended on human effort for their manipulation. Perhaps the popular image of 'Jesus the carpenter' is not quite as romantic as the everyday reality.

Jesus: more than a carpenter

The answer to our starting question 'Is not this the carpenter?' is also 'no', for in the light of the whole Bible, Jesus is infinitely more than a carpenter. He is the unique Son of God—God incarnate; God manifested in the flesh (1 Tim. 3:16), or as the Nicene Creed puts it, 'The only begotten Son of God, begotten of His Father before all worlds, God of God, Light of light, very God of very God, begotten not made, being of one substance with the Father, by whom all things were made, who for us men and for our salvation came down from heaven.'

God incarnate at work

In Christ, Almighty God shared our humanity, sin apart. The Lord Jesus worked as a carpenter. He was no stranger to 'the daily grind'. In Bible times the average working shift was twelve hours (see Matt. 20:1–16). Can you picture the Lord Jesus at work as the perfect craftsman? Can you also picture Him dealing tactfully with the customers for whom He plied His trade? Can you also picture His relief when His busy day came to an end? 'We have not a high priest who is unable to sympathize with our weaknesses' (Heb. 4:15).

The Bible is silent about Jesus' years as a carpenter. In Matthew 11:28–30, though, we read Jesus' wonderful invitation, 'Come to me, all who labor and are heavy laden, and I will give you rest. Take my *yoke* upon you, and learn from me; for I am gentle and lowly in heart, and you will find rest for your souls. For my *yoke* is easy, and my burden is light.' 'Take my *yoke* upon you … my *yoke* is easy.' It is figurative language, of course. It is an invitation to trust the Lord Jesus as our own Saviour and become a lifelong disciple of His. Yet no doubt the Lord Jesus, during His years as a carpenter, would have made actual wooden ox yokes for the farmers who lived in the countryside surrounding Nazareth. He knew the importance of a yoke that fitted well and was comfortable, and so enabled an ox to work pulling the plough with maximum efficiency. His yoke is easy, and His burden is light!

The crucified carpenter

When He was thirty-three years of age, Jesus, the one-time carpenter, became a victim of carpentry. He was Himself nailed to a plank of wood in the gruesome Roman fashion known as crucifixion. A crueller form of capital punishment could not have been devised. Yet it was all according to God's eternal plan of redemption. About 1000 BC, Psalm 22:16–18 foretold Christ's being nailed to the cross. Under the guidance of the Holy Spirit, David was enabled to write an insider's perspective of Calvary: 'they have pierced my hands and feet—I can count all my bones—they stare and gloat over me; they divide my garments among them, and for my raiment they cast lots.'

The cross of Christ takes us to the heart of the Christian faith. Christ died on the cross as the sinner's substitute—to save sinners from the punishment which is their just due from the hands of a holy God. 'He was wounded for *our* transgressions, he was bruised for *our* iniquities,' prophesied Isaiah (Isa. 53:5). He 'was put to death for *our* trespasses', explains Paul (Rom. 4:25).

The carpenter's continued work

Jesus the carpenter thus became nailed to a hideous piece of carpentry for the salvation of His people. The one-time carpenter, however, is now enthroned in heaven, seated at God's right hand in glory. But in one way He is still at work with His carpentry tools. He is working, not on tables and chairs, but on the people He came to redeem. It is the will of God that all who believe in Jesus become more and more like Him—that they grow in holiness, love and Christ-likeness. 'For those whom he foreknew he also predestined to be conformed to the image of his Son' (Rom. 8:29). 'We ... are being changed into his likeness from one degree of glory to another' (2 Cor. 3:18).

How do we become more like Jesus? Through various means. There are the 'means of grace': prayer—that is, spending time with Jesus; reading His Word; and attending a church where His Word is faithfully preached and His ordinances faithfully administered. But the carpenter may also see fit to use His carpentry tools on us to accomplish His purpose. We have many rough edges and flaws that need to be smoothed away and honed. How do we emulate the sympathy of Jesus? How do we deepen our faith in God? These require the chisel of pain, perhaps the hammer of tribulation or maybe the plane of stressful, difficult circumstances. The pressures and frictions of life and the losses and crosses might just be the loving Carpenter's tools at work upon us. He has not finished with us yet! He is working towards a blueprint. He is creating an instrument of righteousness for the glory of God. From unpromising, fallen material, God in Christ is able to fashion wonders beyond all we can imagine—vessels of glory destined for eternal glory.

'Is not this the carpenter?' Yes and no. The Lord Jesus was indeed a carpenter. But the Lord Jesus is infinitely more than a carpenter. An ancient prayer which we could make our own goes as follows:

O Jesus, Master-Carpenter of Nazareth, who on the cross through wood and nails hast wrought man's full salvation, wield well Thy tools in this Thy workshop, that we who come to Thee rough-hewn, may be fashioned into a truer beauty by Thy hand, who with the Father and the Holy Ghost livest and reignest, one God, world without end. Amen.[1]

NOTE

1 Quoted in John Stott, *Your Confirmation* (London: Hodder & Stoughton, 1958), pp. 42–43.

The tanner

In Bible times a 'tanner' did not refer to an old sixpence, nor did it refer to a sunbed. Rather, it referred to a person who tanned animal hides for a living. A tanner was a leather worker—one who made leather from animal hides. Once the leather was produced, it could be used to make everyday objects such as belts, sandal straps and the uppers of shoes—the soles were normally made of wood. Portable bottles for water or wine were also made of leather.

Acts 10–11 describes a time of Christian expansion when the message of the gospel came to Gentile—not just Jewish—converts. It was an epochal moment in God's eternal plan of redemption. Acts 11:18 concludes with the climactic exclamation, 'And they glorified God, saying, "Then to the Gentiles also God has granted repentance unto life"' (Acts 11:18). During this time, Peter was staying at Joppa, on the coast of Israel, and 'lodging with Simon, *a tanner*, whose house is by the seaside' (Acts 10:6).

It was fitting for a tanner's house to be by the sea. Tanning involved the use of animal dung and human urine, the odours of which were quite vile. A sea breeze would disperse these odours. Tanneries in general were thus located outside towns. You would not want to live next door to one! A tanner was often shunned for fear of ritual defilement. His day-to-day job entailed contact with dead animal carcasses. Touching the dead body of either a person or an animal rendered you ceremonially unclean according to the law: 'He who touches the dead body of any person shall be unclean seven days' (Num. 19:11).

Tanning: the process

A tanner would set about his work as follows. First of all, the animal hide was soaked for several days in a mixture of water and human urine. The skins were then cleaned with pure water and stretched out to dry. Once dry, they were scraped with a knife to remove any hair, and then rubbed with a stone and animal dung. Finally, they were hammered soft and flat so that they became malleable and could be worked and forged into the desired object.

Gospel cleanliness

Simon Peter 'stayed in Joppa for many days with one Simon, a tanner' (Acts 9:43). The man was unclean—both separated from his compatriots and separated from God. Peter, though, learned an important lesson: 'What God has cleansed, you must not call common' (Acts 10:15). Ultimately, it is our sin which separates us from God. Our sin defiles us and renders us unfit for God's presence. The gospel, however, provides us with a cleansing from the sin which defiles us—a cleansing available for both Jew and Gentile. 'The blood of Jesus his Son cleanses us from all sin' (1 John 1:7). In Simon the tanner's house, Peter would no doubt have proclaimed the same gospel which he was shortly to proclaim in the house of Cornelius, a Roman centurion: that 'every one who believes in him [that is, Jesus] receives forgiveness of sins through his name' (Acts 10:43).

John the Baptist—Jesus' forerunner—was a beneficiary of the work of a tanner. Scripture records that 'John was clothed with camel's hair, and had a leather girdle around his waist' (Mark 1:6). John, however, said that he was not worthy to touch the leather sandal strap of Jesus' footwear: 'He preached, saying, "After me comes he who is mightier than I, the thong of whose sandals I am not worthy to stoop down and untie"' (Mark 1:7). It was the task of a lowly household servant to remove the sandals of a guest and wash his or her feet. John was saying that he was not worthy even to be Jesus' slave. He was testifying to Jesus' supreme greatness. And Scripture in general attests to the unsurpassed and unsurpassable greatness of the Lord Jesus Christ. He is the Son of God and God the Son. He is the second person of the eternal Trinity. He is co-equal with God the Father and God the Holy Spirit. Worship depends on worth, and there is none worthier than the Lord Jesus. He is the Son of God whom Christians rightly worship. 'For in him the whole fulness of deity dwells bodily' (Col. 2:9).

A leather bottle

We stated earlier that in Bible times, bottles were made from leather. Having a portable bottle of water with you when travelling in the Middle Eastern heat was a great boon. The leather water bottle, however, teaches us spiritual lessons concerning both God's might and his mercy.

HIS MIGHT

God, the great Creator, 'gathered the waters of the sea as in a bottle' (Ps. 33:7). When we consider the vastness of the oceans, we glimpse something of the might of God. Yet the great seas which surround our earthly islands are just water in a bottle to Almighty God. He alone is supremely mighty. He is not bound by our limitations. Nothing is too difficult for Him.

HIS MERCY

In great distress, the psalmist prayed to God, 'Thou hast kept count of my tossings; put thou my tears in thy bottle' (Ps. 56:8). Christians may be assured and reassured that God knows all about every tear we have shed or ever will shed. They are in His bottle. He is our loving, heavenly Father. His Son, the Lord Jesus, is the most sympathetic of Saviours. We are promised the help of the Holy Spirit—the divine comforter—throughout our, at times, tearful earthly life. We have the privilege of turning to God in prayer. 'He cares about you' (1 Peter 5:7). One day, the Bible promises, 'God will wipe away every tear from [our] eyes' (Revelation 7:17).

Chapter 12

The tanner's job was not exactly pleasant, but, once the cleaning and preparation were complete, he produced pleasing and useful results. Amazingly, God takes unclean sinners and, through Christ, transforms them into vessels of His glory.

Fishing

Many of the Lord Jesus' disciples were fishermen. These men lived in the towns surrounding the Sea of Galilee in the north of Israel, and fished its waters for a living. The Sea of Galilee is a freshwater lake some thirteen miles long and seven miles across. In some places it is up to 150 feet deep and even today over twenty different species of fish can be found there. Fish was part of the diet in those days, and it was eaten salted, dried or pickled—the deep freeze was yet a long way off. The fish from the Sea of Galilee provided a valuable livelihood.

In Bible times, fishing was undertaken in various ways. There was the *cast net* or hand net which was usually cast into the lake from the shore. There was also the larger *drag net*. This had floats on the top and weights on the bottom and was thrown into the deeper water from a boat or boats. Fishing using a drag net from a boat was often undertaken at night, when a fisherman would hold a fire lamp to attract the fish to the surface. Fishermen had to be brave, as the Sea of Galilee was and is well known for its sudden storms and squalls. More rarely, fishing was done with a *line and hook* or even a spear. Once a shoal of fish had been netted, it would be hauled to the shore, sorted and counted—tax having to be paid on the catch—and then taken to the market to be sold. When the fishermen were not out fishing, they could be found cleaning and mending their nets on the shore and ensuring that their boat was in working order.

Fishing for souls

In Matthew 4 we read, 'As he [the Lord Jesus] walked by the Sea of Galilee, he saw two brothers, Simon who is called Peter and Andrew his brother, casting a net into the sea; for they were fishermen. And he said to them, "Follow me, and I will make you fishers of men." Immediately they left their nets and followed him' (vv. 18–20).

These Galilean fishermen were called to exchange fishing for fish for fishing for the souls of men and women. It reminds us that the Christian faith is an active, evangelistic faith. It seeks to 'catch' men and women in the net of the gospel of saving grace. However, whereas fish are caught and then die, men and women who are, by nature, spiritually dead (Eph. 2:1), once netted by the gospel, are caught and then begin to live, for 'the free gift of God is eternal life in Christ Jesus our Lord' (Rom. 6:23).

Fishing in the Sea of Galilee necessitated courage, faith, team work and perseverance. No doubt these qualities which the early fishermen disciples had developed through their trade were sanctified by God for greater use. Fishing for souls also requires courage, faith, team work and perseverance. God can use what we have—just as Christ fed more than five thousand people from five loaves and two fish which a young boy had brought with him for his lunch—and then sanctify and extend it for work in the kingdom of heaven. Ephesians 3:20 reads, 'Now to him who by the power at work within us is able to do far more abundantly than all that we ask or think.'

Following Jesus

Jesus said, 'Follow me!' to these Galilean fishermen. The Gospels record that 'Immediately they left their nets and followed him' (Matt. 4:20). Elijah once issued the challenge to the people of Israel: 'If the LORD is God, follow him' (1 Kings 18:21). Here we have a pointer to Christ's deity. Who but God can demand and require our total obedience and allegiance? Jesus still calls us to follow Him wholeheartedly:

Jesus calls us: o'er the tumult
Of our life's wild, restless sea;

Day by day His sweet voice soundeth
Saying, 'Christian, follow me.'

As of old, apostles heard it
By the Galilean lake,
Turned from home and toil and kindred
Leaving all for His dear sake.[1]

Fishing miracles

The Lord Jesus was originally a carpenter by trade, not a fisherman. However, the Bible reveals that on two occasions He enabled His fishermen disciples to catch a miraculous haul of fish. At the beginning of Jesus' public ministry, Peter sighed that 'we toiled all night and took nothing!' (Luke 5:5). Notwithstanding, Jesus commanded him, 'Put out into the deep and let down your nets for a catch' (5:4). 'And when they had done this, they enclosed a great shoal of fish; and … their nets were breaking' (5:6). Then John 21 relates how the risen Christ stood on the shore of Lake Galilee at dawn and called to His disciples who were out fishing in their boat, about a hundred yards off the shore, saying,

'Children, have you any fish?' They answered him, 'No.' He said to them, 'Cast the net on the right side of the boat, and you will find some.' So they cast it, and now they were not able to haul it in, for the quantity of fish … Simon Peter … hauled the net ashore, full of large fish, a hundred and fifty-three of them (John 21:5–6, 11).

Earlier in His ministry, Jesus had enabled Peter to catch just one fish miraculously—a fish known as a 'Talipia'—with a line and hook. They both needed to pay the temple tax. Peter, at Jesus' word, cast a hook into the sea and … the first fish he caught had just the right coin in its mouth for them to be able to pay the temple tax. The miracle reveals Jesus' absolute providential control. Someone had to lose a coin. The coin had to end up in the lake. A certain fish had to put the coin in the pouch in its mouth. Peter had to catch that particular fish at its first 'bite'. Peter's catching of the fish with the coin simply cannot be explained by human engineering.

The last Adam

The 'fishing miracles' of Jesus reveal His lordship over the animal world—the crown rights of the Creator over His creation. Genesis 2 reveals that Adam originally had dominion over the animal kingdom, although this was lost when sin entered the world. Christ's dominion over the animal kingdom is a facet of His being 'the last Adam'. Psalm 8:6–8 applies to Him: 'Thou hast given him dominion over the works of thy hands; thou hast put all things under his feet, all sheep and oxen, and also the beasts of the field, the birds of the air, and *the fish of the sea*, whatever passes along the paths of the sea.' Jesus is 'the second Adam' who 'to the fight and to the rescue came'. He came to undo the ravages of sin wrought through Adam, our first ancestor.

The last judgement

Finally, we note that the Lord Jesus used familiar fishing practice and imagery in one of His parables—the 'Parable of the Drag Net'. In Matthew 13:47–50 He said,

The kingdom of heaven is like a net which was thrown into the sea and gathered fish of every kind; when it was full, men drew it ashore and sat down and sorted the good into vessels but threw away the bad. So it will be at the close of the age. The angels will come out and separate the evil from the righteous, and throw them into the furnace of fire; there men will weep and gnash their teeth.

The parable is formidable and searching. It points to the end of the age when there will be a great divide between the saved and the unsaved—the righteous and the condemned. One group will spend eternity in the bliss of heaven—but the other will spend eternity in the flames of hell. The parable has an evangelistic thrust. It causes us to ask ourselves, 'In which category or group do I and will I fit?' The gospel tells us that if we belong to Jesus, we need not fear the judgement to come. Jesus has saved us from the flames of hell! The Bible assures us, 'There is therefore now no condemnation for those who are in Christ Jesus' (Rom. 8:1).

NOTE

1   Cecil F. Alexander, 'Jesus Calls Us'.

The silver-refiner

In Proverbs 17:3 we read, 'The crucible is for silver, and the furnace is for gold, and the LORD tries hearts.' Similarly, in Malachi 3:3 we read that God will 'sit as a refiner and purifier of silver'.

The silver-refining industry was well known in Bible times. The silver-refiner sat at his work. He would fan his charcoal fire as he looked intently into his crucible containing molten metal. He would wait patiently until he saw a clear reflection of his face in the liquid metal below. When his face appeared clearly, he would be satisfied. The heat had done its work. The dross and impurities had been burnt away and the metal was now useable and useful. It could be used to make something special—perhaps a chalice or a candlestick. 'Take away the dross from the silver, and the smith has material for a vessel' (Prov. 25:4).

The divine refiner

Refining silver is one thing, but the Bible, in the verses quoted, suggests that God refines His people. He turns up the heat upon them. It is one of the ways in which we may view the various trials and difficulties that God sends into our lives in His providence. They are part of His process of sanctification—a process that will not be complete until a reflection of the face of Jesus is seen in us.

Almighty God continues to refine His people. He does so, not to save them, because God's people are already saved—saved by the Christ who went through the suffering of Calvary on their behalf. No. God refines His people to sanctify them—to get rid of the remaining dross that hinders our spiritual usefulness; to get rid of those blemishes that mar our Christ-likeness. The process is a long, slow, painful one for sure, and it will never be complete in this life. One day, however, it will be perfectly complete, for 'He who began a good work in you will bring it to completion at the day of Jesus Christ' (Phil. 1:6). Trials are painful. Yet how good it is to know that our God of infinite love, wisdom and righteousness is the one controlling the temperature of the trials which come into our lives! It is wise, therefore, to submit to God's refining and cooperate with Him as best we can. An ageing Paul wrote to young Timothy in 2 Timothy 2:21–22, 'If any one purifies himself from what is ignoble, then he will be a vessel for noble use, consecrated and useful to the master of the house, ready for any good work. So shun youthful passions and aim at righteousness, faith, love, and peace, along with those who call upon the Lord from a pure heart.' Oh to be a vessel fit for the Master's use, one that is useable, useful and glorifying to God and a channel of His blessing to others!

The heat is on!

'The crucible is for silver, and the furnace is for gold, and the LORD tries hearts' (Prov. 17:3). No one would ever suggest that being in God's crucible is pleasant. It may be necessary, for sure, as sin is so deeply ingrained in us. It may also have a wonderful end result and so be ultimately worthwhile. Yet when the heat is on, our maturity or otherwise is revealed. Often, it is not how we act but how we *re*act that reveals our true character.

The painful nature of being in God's crucible—along with the beneficial end result—was known all too well to the writer of the epistle to the Hebrews, a letter written to some believers who were living through difficult times. Using the illustration of a loving father being 'cruel to be kind' and disciplining his son, the writer said the following definitive words concerning divine chastisement:

'My son, do not regard lightly the discipline of the Lord,
nor lose courage when you are punished by him.

For the Lord disciplines him whom he loves,
and chastises every son whom he receives.'

… God is treating you as sons; for what son is there whom his father does not discipline? … He disciplines us for our good, that we may share his holiness. For the moment all discipline seems painful rather than pleasant; later it yields the peaceful fruit of righteousness to those who have been trained by it (Heb. 12:5–7, 10–11).

The non-Christian world would have difficulty understanding that the trials and difficulties of a Christian's life are evidence of God's love, but they are! God is refining His silver! He will have His way. He has not finished with us yet. He is making us more like Jesus. 'The LORD will fulfil his purpose for me; thy steadfast love, O LORD, endures for ever. Do not forsake the work of thy hands' (Ps. 138:8).

So when troubles, trials, pains and perplexities come your way, seek the Lord and His grace. And remember that our Father in heaven is a silver-refiner *par excellence*. He promises,

When through fiery trials thy pathway shall lie,
My grace all-sufficient shall be thy supply;
The flame shall not hurt thee; I only design
Thy dross to consume, and thy gold to refine.[1]

NOTE

1   'How Firm a Foundation', from *A Selection of Hymns by John Rippon*.

The eastern shepherd

A shepherd and his sheep were a common sight in the land of the Bible. The Good News of the birth of 'a Savior, who is Christ the Lord' (Luke 2:11) was first announced on the outskirts of Bethlehem to some 'shepherds out in the field, keeping watch over their flock by night' (Luke 2:8). David, Israel's greatest king, was originally a shepherd before God 'took him from the sheepfolds; from tending the ewes that had young he brought him to be the shepherd of Jacob his people' (Ps. 78:70–71). Sheep and goats were bred for meat, milk, clothing and temple sacrifice.

The famous psalm

David used his experience as a shepherd to write the most famous psalm of all—Psalm 23. The psalm begins, 'The LORD is my shepherd, I shall not want' (Ps. 23:1), and then unfolds what this affirmation means in practice. The chief task and concern of the shepherd was simple and overriding: the welfare of his sheep—ensuring that they did not 'want' for anything. This involved leading them to 'green pastures'. The eastern shepherd always led, rather than drive, his sheep. 'He goes before them, and the sheep follow him, for they know his voice' (John 10:4). The 'green pastures' refer to scrubland—pastureland suitable for grazing sheep. Food was essential for the flock's welfare. The shepherd thus ensured that the green pastures were safe for the sheep. He would kill any snakes and clear it of stones and thorn bushes. Pastureland was also known as 'tableland'. This preparation of the tableland underlies the verse 'Thou preparest a table before me in the presence of my enemies' (Ps. 23:5).

Water was also vital for the sheep's welfare in the hot Middle East. The shepherd would lead his flock 'beside still waters' (Ps. 23:2). Rushing water would frighten the sheep. A sheep's anatomy is such that its mouth and nose are close together, so fast-moving water might cause it to choke. A shepherd would thus lead his sheep to 'still waters' where they could drink and be revived. 'He restores my soul' (Ps. 23:3).

Feeding, leading, guarding, guiding …

The shepherd knew the lie of the land. He knew the location of the green pastures and the still waters, and he would lead his sheep to them. 'He leads me in right paths [margin] for his name's sake' (Ps. 23:3). The reputation of the shepherd was bound up with the welfare of his sheep. His leading might, though, have necessitated their passing through dark and dangerous valleys. Sheep are timid—but as long as the shepherd was with them, they would feel safe. 'Even though I walk through the valley of the shadow of death, I fear no evil; for thou art with me' (Ps. 23:4).

The shepherd had a 'rod' and 'staff' (Ps. 23:4) and would use them if necessary. The rod was a club—an offensive weapon—to ward off those who attacked the sheep. The staff gently guided the sheep and could be used to rescue them if they slipped down a valley. At the day's end, the shepherd would lead his sheep into the safety of a sheepfold or pen. He would stand at its opening and the sheep would 'pass under the rod' (Ezek. 20:37). As they did so, he would count them. If even just one was missing, he would go and search for it and bring it back to the fold. This gives us the background to the Lord Jesus' 'Parable of the Lost Sheep' in Luke 15. The shepherd would also inspect each sheep. If any had grazes on their heads or traces of sunburn, he would anoint their heads with oil to soothe their discomfort. If any seemed lethargic, he would give them a drink from his water bottle—'Thou anointest my head with oil, my cup overflows' (Ps. 23:5). The sheep would stay the night in the safety of the sheepfold, accompanied by the shepherd. The sheepfold was communal: more than one shepherd and flock would share it. In the morning, though, the shepherd would call his own flock out of the fold, and the leading and feeding would begin once more. 'The sheep hear his voice, and he calls his own sheep by name and leads them out' (John 10:3).

The Good Shepherd

In John 10:11 Jesus stated, 'I am the good shepherd.' We must be careful not to over-sentimentalize this claim. Actually, it was a claim to deity. Psalm 23:1 reads, 'The LORD is my shepherd.' Jesus was thus claiming co-equality with God. He was also teaching that all that applies to a good shepherd and his sheep applies to Him and His followers. He has our eternal welfare at heart. We may trust Him. He will lead us. He will feed us. He will guard us. He will guide us. He will undertake for us. We may be assured that He will never fail us nor forsake us. Jesus is a shepherd of infinite vigilance and tender care.

He then went on to say, 'The good shepherd lays down his life for the sheep' (John 10:11). And Jesus did indeed. This takes us to the cross of Calvary, where Jesus died in our place to save us. Paradoxically, the Shepherd became a sacrificial Lamb.

The famous shepherd psalm ends with the confident words 'I shall dwell in the house of the LORD for ever' (Ps. 23:6). If we belong to Jesus, the Good Shepherd, we are assured of a place in God's house. Heaven is a prepared place for a prepared people. The sacrifice of Christ at Calvary has made us fit for heaven. Amazingly, though, Jesus is also currently preparing heaven for us! He said, 'In my Father's house are many rooms; if it were not so, would I have told you that I go to prepare a place for you?' (John 14:2).

The shepherd and his sheep therefore give us the most wonderful illustration of the reality of our relationship with God in Christ—the relationship between the sinner and his or her Saviour. 'We are his people, and the sheep of his pasture' (Ps. 100:3). If the Lord God really is our Shepherd—if we are united to Christ by saving faith—it is inconceivable that we should ever want for anything, in time or eternity.

Chapter 15

The King of love my Shepherd is,
Whose goodness faileth never;
I nothing lack if I am His,
And He is mine for ever.[1]

NOTE

1 Henry Williams Baker, 'The King of Love My Shepherd Is'.

A Roman soldier's armour

Iirst-century Israel during the time of Christ was under Roman occupation. This had its pros and cons. The Romans kept the peace on land and sea, and gave both Jews and Christians a degree of liberty to practise their faith. Yet being under the government of a pagan power grated on some of the Jews. The sight of the Roman Standard—the Roman Imperial eagle—being paraded was very alien to them. There were some, known as the Zealots, who were all for rising up and overthrowing Rome by force of arms. The Roman soldier on patrol was a common sight during New Testament times.

The Bible reveals that there were some in the first-century Roman army who came to saving faith in Christ. Cornelius, 'a centurion of what was known as the Italian Cohort' (Acts 10:1), was one of these believers. He came to salvation through the ministry of the Apostle Peter—see Acts 10–11. Then Paul, when imprisoned in Rome, was guarded by a group of soldiers. Paul saw himself as 'an ambassador in chains' (Eph. 6:20) and employed the opportunity to tell the soldiers about the Saviour. God blessed his witness, for Paul wrote to the church at Philippi, 'I want you to know, brethren, that what has happened to me has really served to advance the gospel, so that it has become known throughout the whole praetorian guard … that my imprisonment is for Christ' (Phil. 1:12–13).

Whilst imprisoned and under the guard of a Roman soldier, Paul—aided by the Holy Spirit—employed a sanctified imagination. He observed the Roman soldier's armour, and it gave him an illustration of the spiritual armour which God gives to every Christian for the spiritual battle we face in the world. We will need this armour until we reach heaven. Only then will the battle be over and we can 'lay down our sword'.

The armour which God provides is not just to be admired: Paul urges every believer to actually *use* this armour: 'Be strong in the Lord and in the strength of his might. Put on the whole armor of God, that you may be able to stand against the wiles of the devil' (Eph. 6:10–11). This divine armour consists of six pieces. The details of these are found in Ephesians 6:10–20. Again, we stress that this armour is not to be displayed but to wear and use. Paul exhorts, 'Therefore take the whole armor of God' (Eph. 6:13). Let us consider this armour further:

The belt

'Stand therefore, having girded your loins with truth,' says Paul (Eph. 6:14). He was referring to the Roman soldier's belt which held his sword. The implication is that the soldier is on guard, alert and ready for enemy attack. In the spiritual war, Paul says, it is the truth of God which enables us to overcome the attacks of the enemy. Paul is referring to the revealed truth of God. 'Thy word is truth' (John 17:17). Jesus said, 'I am the way, and the *truth*, and the life' (John 14:6). When doubts arise, then, we remind ourselves of the truth of God's Word. Our sin notwithstanding, in the Bible we are assured of the love and mercy of God to us in Christ. This being so, truly all is well with us, for 'If God is for us, who is against us?' (Rom. 8:31).

The breastplate

'... And having put on the breastplate of righteousness' (Eph. 6:14). The soldier's breastplate protected his chest and heart, and covered his body from the neck to the top of the thighs. The Christian likewise is 'covered' with the righteousness of Christ—His 'imputed' righteousness. This alone enables us to 'stand' before both the devil's accusations and God's judgement throne. Our righteousness is not intrinsic to us, but given to us as a gift of God in Christ—'not having a righteousness of my own, based on law, but that which is through faith in Christ; the righteousness from

God that depends on faith' (Phil. 3:8). The technical term for this is 'justification'. 'Justification is an act of God's free grace, wherein he pardoneth all our sins, and accepteth us as righteous in his sight, only for the righteousness of Christ imputed to us, and received by faith alone' ('Westminster Shorter Catechism', answer to Q. 33).

The shoes

'... And having shod your feet with the equipment of the gospel of peace' (Eph. 6:15). A Roman soldier's shoes are best described as 'hob-nailed sandals'—sandals with nails in the soles. These gave him the necessary stability in hand-to-hand fighting and aided his mobility when travelling on land by foot. In our spiritual warfare, 'the gospel of peace', Paul states, is akin to the special shoes of a Roman soldier. 'We have peace with God through our Lord Jesus Christ' (Rom. 5:1) through His 'making peace by the blood of his cross' (Col. 1:20). This peace is unchanged and unchanging, for nothing can undo the finished work of Christ at Calvary. Here is the only true source of stability in a changing world. 'Jesus Christ is the same yesterday and today and for ever' (Heb. 13:8). The cross of Christ gives us eternal peace with God—a peace which transcends this life and enables us to move from earth to heaven with anticipation rather than fear.

The shield

'Besides all these, taking the shield of faith, with which you can quench all the flaming darts of the evil one' (Eph. 6:16). A Roman soldier's shield was large and offered protection from enemy arrows. It was made of wood and covered with leather. The leather was moistened, so when a flaming arrow was fired at him, the shield would put out the flame.

Faith in God, Paul says, puts out the enemy's fiery darts. When things are difficult, by faith we remember that our God is in control. When we feel unworthy, by faith we remember that we are clothed with the perfect righteousness of Christ. Faith in God—in His goodness, providence and redemption, as revealed in His Word—is more than a match for Satan's darts. The faith Paul is referring to here is not so much saving faith but active, ongoing faith in God's wisdom, love, providence and power, remembering, 'Shall not the Judge of all the earth do right?' (Gen. 18:25), and 'with God nothing will be impossible' (Luke 1:37).

The helmet

'And take the helmet of salvation' (Eph. 6:17). A Roman soldier's helmet gave vital protection to his head and brain. The assurance of our salvation gives the Christian peace of mind. In 1 Thessalonians 5:8 Paul entreats, 'Let us be sober, and put on the breastplate of faith and love, and for a helmet the hope of salvation.' Our 'hope' of salvation is not an uncertain, 'hope so' hope. Rather, it is a confident assurance based on the promises of God in Christ. God keeps His promises. We thus have the 'hope of eternal life which God, who never lies, promised ages ago' (Titus 1:2).

'Salvation' is an all-embracing word. It means rescue or deliverance and much more. In Christ we are saved from the wrath of God. In Christ we are rescued from hell. But in Christ we are also reconciled to God. In Christ we know blessed fellowship with God here and hereafter. In Christ we have an all-embracing salvation—forgiveness, justification, adoption, eternal life, the 'hope of glory' and so much more!

The sword

'... And the sword of the Spirit, which is the word of God' (Eph. 6:17). The soldier's sword was an offensive weapon rather than a defensive protection. He would employ it in close fighting. God's Word is likened to a sword: 'The word of God is living and active, sharper than any two-edged sword' (Heb. 4:12). It was by this sword that the Lord Jesus repelled Satan in the wilderness. Three times He quoted at him, 'It is written ...' And the Redeemer here gives the redeemed an example to emulate. We may repel Satan by quoting the promises of God in the Bible at him.

The story is told that Martin Luther once envisioned Satan writing all his sins and faults on the wall, seeking to cause Luther to doubt his salvation. How could God's child think, do or say such things? Luther repelled Satan by the Word of God. Through all the sins written on the wall, he wrote one verse: 'the blood of Jesus his Son cleanses us from all sin' (1 John 1:7).

The Christian life is a battleground, not a playground—and will be so until we reach glory. But God has given us gospel armour to wear. He has given us the Lord Jesus Christ. 'Put on the Lord Jesus Christ' (Rom. 13:14). Every piece of the armour ultimately directs us to Jesus. He is the truth, our righteousness, our peace, the object of our faith, our hope of salvation and the One to whom the Word of God directs us. The incarnate Word and the inspired Word are one. Through Christ and His Word we are victorious. 'We are more than conquerors through him who loved us' (Rom. 8:37).

Soldiers of Christ, arise,
And put your armour on,
Strong in the strength which God supplies
Through His eternal Son.[1]

NOTE

1   Charles Wesley, 'Soldiers of Christ, Arise'.

The temple

In the time of Christ, the city of Jerusalem was dominated by one building: the temple. The temple was central to Israel's religious life. The temple was a place of worship, but primarily it was a place of animal sacrifice. Blood sacrifice was integral to the religious economy of Israel.

Sacrifice was ordained by God Himself as a means of approaching Him and atoning for human sin. Sin against God is so serious that it deserves to be punished by death, but God allowed the death of an innocent animal to be accepted in the place of the sinner who brought the sacrifice. Leviticus 17:11 is a key verse of the Bible. Here God Himself explains, 'For the life of the flesh is in the blood; and I have given it for you upon the altar to make atonement for your souls; for it is the blood that makes atonement, by reason of the life.'

The history of the temple

The first temple in Jerusalem was built under the leadership of King Solomon in about 965 BC. It was sited on the threshing floor of one Araunah the Jebusite on the mountain top of Mount Moriah, where Abraham had built an altar to sacrifice his son Isaac a century or so previously (see 2 Chr. 3:1 and Gen. 22). The temple was a permanent and more ornate version of the portable tabernacle dating from the time of Moses, and its design was patterned on the tabernacle. It had an outer court in which stood the altar of burnt offering and a 'laver' for washing. The central shrine was divided into the Holy Place and the 'Holy of Holies'. In the Holy Place stood a seven-branched lamp stand, an altar of incense and a table of 'shewbread'. In the Holy of Holies stood the Ark of the Covenant, which contained the two stone tablets of the law of Moses.

This special box was overlaid with pure gold. Its lid formed the 'mercy seat' on which were two golden cherubim. The Holy of Holies was indeed holy, for God Himself manifested His presence there in a special, particular and localized way. Hence only the high priest was permitted to enter this place, and only once a year, on the annual Day of Atonement, and only with the blood of a sacrificial offering which was sprinkled on the mercy seat.

Solomon's temple was destroyed by the Babylonians in 587 BC. At that time, the Jews were taken into exile. Seventy years later, however, under Persian rule, they were permitted to return to Jerusalem and rebuild the temple. After some fits and starts, the temple was eventually rebuilt. 'And the people of Israel, the priests and the Levites, and the rest of the returned exiles, celebrated the dedication of this house of God with joy' (Ezra 6:16). The Holy of Holies at this time, however, did not contain the Ark of the Covenant. This was lost or destroyed during the Babylonian conquest. It was represented by a block of black stone.

When Herod the Great came to power in 19 BC, hoping to ingratiate himself with the Jewish people, he began a rebuilding, renovation, extension and expansion of the second temple which stood in Jerusalem. The central shrine was finished in 9 BC, but the work on the outer buildings and courts continued afterwards. This ongoing building work was the scene at the time of Christ. Hence we read the Jews' remark to Jesus, 'It has taken forty-six years to build this temple' (John 2:20).

The temple, then, was a place of sacrifice, but also a place of divine worship and teaching. All devout Jews in Bible times would have been familiar with its precincts. The law of Moses required them to visit the temple three times a year: 'Three times a year all your males shall appear before the LORD your God at the place which he will choose: at the feast of unleavened bread [Passover], at the feast of weeks [Pentecost], and at the feast of booths [Tabernacles]' (Deut. 16:16).

The temple and Jesus

Significantly, the first-recorded words of the Lord Jesus were spoken when He visited Jerusalem with His family during the Feast of the Passover. He was just twelve years of age, and his parents had lost him. They searched anxiously for Him and found Him in the outer temple courts conversing with teachers. When Mary His mother said to Him, 'Behold, your father and I have been looking for you anxiously' (Luke 2:48), He replied, 'Did you not know that I must be in my Father's house?' (Luke 2:49). These first-recorded words of Jesus reveal His unique, divine sonship. He was aware that He was the one and only Son of God even at that tender age.

The temple at Jerusalem was an awesome, imposing building which dominated the Jerusalem skyline. Once, the Bible records, 'as he [Jesus] came out of the temple, one of his disciples said to him, "Look, Teacher, what wonderful stones and what wonderful buildings!"'(Mark 13:1). The Lord Jesus did not disagree. Yet He went on to prophesy the destruction of the temple—and in AD 70, under the Roman general Titus, His prophecy was fulfilled. The Roman armies destroyed the temple. All that is left of it today is the outer, western wall, known as the 'wailing wall'. From a Christian point of view, however, this is not a tragedy, for the temple is now no longer needed, having served its purpose in God's economy. Jesus' once-for-all sacrifice of Himself at Calvary has rendered the temple and its sacrifices obsolete. Rebuilding it would undermine the perfection of Christ's finished work.

The synagogue

Luke 4:16 reports that, when visiting His home town of Nazareth, Jesus 'went to the *synagogue*, as His custom was, on the Sabbath day'. The word 'synagogue' means 'a coming together'. It refers to the building in which Jews assemble for worship and instruction. In Bible times synagogues were scattered throughout the land of Israel and the wider Graeco-Roman world.

The consensus is that the synagogue originated during the time of the Babylonian exile. At that time, the people of Israel were exiled out of the Promised Land and their beloved temple—the focal point of their faith— had been destroyed. In Babylon they used to meet together on the Sabbath day, read the Scriptures they had and pray to God. Humanly speaking, the synagogue went a long way towards keeping the faith alive. The institution and practices of the synagogue continued after the exile in the Diaspora—the scattering of Jews throughout the world. In any town or village, if there was a minimum of ten Jewish men, a synagogue was formed and Jewish public worship was undertaken. Public worship in the synagogue always began with the 'Shema'—what could be considered as the basic creed of Judaism. The Shema is contained in Deuteronomy 6:4–5: 'Hear, O Israel: The LORD our God is one LORD; and you shall love the LORD your God with all your heart, and with all your soul, and with all your might.'

Synagogue layout
The design of a synagogue was very simple. In the middle of the room was a raised platform or *bimah*. From here the service was conducted by the service leader or rabbi. In Bible days, people sat on benches or mats on the floor and the seating was arranged so that all faced the *bimah*. In

Bible days men and women sat separately. In a special cupboard—or 'ark'—on the eastern wall which faced Jerusalem, the scrolls of the Scriptures were kept. In front of this ark a lamp was kept burning continuously. The physical light was symbolic of the spiritual light of the Scriptures: 'Thy word is a lamp to my feet and a light to my path' (Ps. 119:105). Whilst the synagogue served mainly as a focus for worship on the Sabbath and at festival time, its building was multi-functional. It also served as a schoolroom for Jewish boys and as a community centre.

Jesus and the synagogue

References to the synagogue in relation to the ministry of the Lord Jesus abound in the New Testament. In Capernaum, for instance, 'on the sabbath he entered the synagogue and taught' (Mark 1:21). He then proceeded to exorcise an unclean spirit from a man, bringing him physical and spiritual transformation. Mark 3:1–5 records how, in the synagogue, Jesus healed a man who had a withered, useless hand.

Three times in the Gospels, Jesus is recorded as bringing the dead back to life. One of these deceased persons was the twelve-year-old daughter of Jairus. Jairus is described as 'one of the rulers of the synagogue' (Mark 5:22). In Luke 7:1–10 we read of Jesus healing a centurion's slave. Unusually, the slave was healed from a distance, not by physical contact. The centurion himself, being Roman, was not Jewish by birth. However, his sympathy for Judaism is gleaned from the description of him that 'he loves our nation, and he built us our synagogue' (Luke 7:5).

Scripture records that Jesus was once expelled from His home synagogue in Nazareth. His intrinsic authority was such that He was asked to lead the service there on the Sabbath day. He chose to read from the prophet Isaiah. Luke records,

He opened the book and found the place where it was written,
'The Spirit of the Lord is upon me,

because he has anointed me to preach good news to the poor.
He has sent me to proclaim release to the captives
and recovering of sight to the blind,
to set at liberty those who are oppressed,
to proclaim the acceptable year of the Lord' …

The eyes of all in the synagogue were fixed on him. And he began to say to them, 'Today this scripture has been fulfilled in your hearing' (Luke 4:17–19, 20–21).

Jesus' audacious claim angered the congregation in Nazareth—though with hindsight, we can see that He was speaking the plain truth. Jesus is the longed-for Messiah—the 'anointed one'. He brings the salvation of God. He is the Good News. He bestows the riches of God's grace on poor sinners. He brings redemption—freedom from the penalty and power of sin. He is the One to whom all Scripture points—the key to unlock the whole Bible. The inhabitants of the synagogue in Nazareth took this badly and tried to kill Jesus—but the truth still stood.

Christian mission

When we turn to the Acts of the Apostles, we see that the early Christian evangelists frequented the Jewish synagogue. They did not go there primarily to worship, however. Rather, they used the synagogue as a launching pad for the gospel of Christ. Paul and Silas, for instance,

came to Thessalonica, where there was a synagogue of the Jews. And Paul went in, as was his custom, and for three weeks he argued with them from the scriptures, explaining and proving that it was necessary for the Christ to suffer and to rise from the dead, and saying, 'This Jesus, whom I proclaim to you, is the Christ' (Acts 17:1–3).

The message of Paul was therefore the same as the message of Jesus: the longed-for Messiah has come; He died and rose again for the salvation of sinners; we must respond to Him in repentance and faith.

The synagogue and the church

The synagogue was therefore a well-known institution in Bible times. Christians, however, do not worship in a synagogue on the seventh day, but gather 'in church' in the name of Jesus on the first day—our Sunday. The church grew out of the synagogue, and the church is inexplicable apart from the cross and empty tomb of Christ.

A. M. Renwick comments,

The worship of the early church was modelled upon the simple service of the synagogue rather than upon the ritualistic service of the temple, and the worshippers really came into vital touch with God. The result was a most powerful and effective Church. We are astonished at what they accomplished. With no worldly grandeur, with little social influence, without even church buildings, these early Christians went on from strength to strength, in spite of the opposition of the great Roman Empire and the bitter animosity of a sinful, pagan world which hated them.[1]

The Christian life is akin to synagogue life in that it is communal. The New Testament urges Christians, 'Let us consider how to stir up one another to love and good works, not neglecting to meet together, as is the habit of some, but encouraging one another' (Heb. 10:24–25). The Christian church is distinguished from other societies by the special presence of Christ in her midst. Jesus promised, 'For where two or three are gathered in my name, there am I in the midst of them' (Matt. 18:20). Christians gather in the name of Jesus to worship Him, hear His Word and remember His saving death in the way He ordained—by eating bread and drinking wine. Such occasions can be a foretaste of heaven, for Jesus Himself is in our midst!

With Jesus in our midst
We gather round the board
Though many, we are one in Christ
One body in the Lord. [2]

NOTES

1   A. M. Renwick, *The Story of the Church* (Leicester: IVP, 1996), p. 22.
2   R. C. Chapman, 'With Jesus in Our Midst'.

The Sabbath

Life in Bible times was physically demanding and tiring. Our modern conveniences—such as electricity, cars and advanced medicine—were all unknown in those days. Yet God's people were never more than a week away from a welcome break and holiday—a true 'holy day'. We refer to the Sabbath day. The word 'Sabbath' comes from the Hebrew verb 'to rest or cease'. The Sabbath was a commandment of God ordained for His people's blessing and benefit. It was a means of physical rest and refreshment and spiritual renewal.

The fourth commandment, given by God to Moses, stipulated, 'Remember the sabbath day, to keep it holy. Six days you shall labor, and do all your work; but the seventh day is a sabbath to the LORD your God; in it you shall not do any work' (Exod. 20:8–10). Whilst the Sabbath commandment was codified in the time of Moses, however, the origin of the Sabbath predates Moses and goes back to the dawn of world history. Almighty God Himself is revealed as resting on the seventh day, having completed His creation of the universe in the preceding six days: 'And on the seventh day God finished his work which he had done, and he rested on the seventh day from all his work which he had done. So God blessed the seventh day and hallowed it, because on it God rested from all his work which he had done in creation' (Gen. 2:2–3).

A holy day

The Sabbath was and is a gracious provision of God for His people's welfare. It is a 'holy day'—that is, a different, special or separate day. It is a day devoted to God, when His people specifically turn from the things of earth to the things of God—from changing, temporal matters to permanent, eternal matters: 'the seventh day is a sabbath of solemn rest, *holy to the* LORD' (Exod. 31:15). Calvin writes,

> By means of the rest of the seventh day, the Lord wished to represent to the people of Israel the spiritual rest by which believers must cease from their own works in order to let the Lord do His work in them. Secondly, He wished that there should be established a definite day in which believers might assemble to hear His Law and engage in worshipping Him.[1]

The Sabbath day therefore keeps us in spiritual 'focus'. It prevents our being so unduly bound up in the everyday concerns of eating, drinking and working that Almighty God, our Maker and Redeemer, is sidelined and forgotten.

The Sabbath is a reminder that this world is here solely because it was created by God: 'Remember the sabbath day, to keep it holy … for in six days the LORD made heaven and earth, the sea, and all that is in them, and rested the seventh day; therefore the LORD blessed the sabbath day and hallowed it' (Exod. 20:8, 11).

The Sabbath is also a reminder of God's saving grace and goodness. He is the redeemer of His people. He has intervened for our salvation. 'Observe the sabbath day, to keep it holy … You shall remember that you were a servant in the land of Egypt, and the LORD your God brought you out thence with a mighty hand and an outstretched arm; therefore the LORD your God commanded you to keep the sabbath day' (Deut. 5:12, 15).

On the Sabbath day, the public and private worship of God is to take precedence. The Bible reveals Him as both the great Creator and a gracious Redeemer, infinitely worthy of His people's devotion. God's people are distinguished from others by being the special objects of His saving grace. God's people are thus to distinguish themselves from others by devoting the whole of their lives to God generally, and by keeping one day in seven specifically, devoted to His special service. God said of this day, 'It is a sign for ever between me and the people of Israel' (Exod. 31:17).

We tend to think that a new day begins at either midnight or dawn. The Sabbath day, however, began at sunset on what we would consider 'the day before'—our Friday. The origin of this again goes back to the creation account in Genesis, where we read the refrain, 'And there was evening and there was morning, one day' (Gen. 1:5 etc.). Blasts of a ram's horn signalled that the Sabbath day had arrived. In Bible times, the day was observed strictly: 'in it you shall not do any work.' During the wilderness wanderings of the people of Israel, we read that God wonderfully provided a double portion of bread—manna—for His people the day before the Sabbath. This enabled them to keep the Sabbath commandment (see Exod. 16). Normally, the provision of manna was enough for only one day, and if it was hoarded for the next day it went off. On the Sabbath day, though, it miraculously lasted for two days (Exod. 16:24).

In Isaiah 58:13 God says, 'If you turn back your foot from the sabbath, from doing your pleasure on my holy day, and call the sabbath a delight …' Joy in the Lord was at the heart of the Sabbath. 'This is the day which the LORD has made; let us rejoice and be glad in it' (Ps. 118:24). As time went on, however, the joy of the Sabbath was marred by legalism. The Jewish leaders added more and more prohibitions and stipulations to God's commandment, with the honest motive of 'putting a hedge around the law'. The Lord Jesus kept the Sabbath, but broke the man-made traditions that had been built up around it. To the consternation of the Jewish religious leaders, He performed miracles of healing on the Sabbath day, and explained, 'My Father is working still, and I am working' (John 5:17). Christian consensus teaches that works of necessity and mercy are permitted and even encouraged on the Sabbath day, as the God of the Bible is compassionate to His creatures every day, and it is hypocritical for us to be less so at any time, let alone on God's special day. When the Lord Jesus healed a man's withered hand on the Sabbath day, He asked some Pharisees, 'What man of you, if he has one sheep and it falls into a pit on the sabbath, will not lay hold of it and lift it out? Of how much more value is a man than a sheep! So it is lawful to do good on the sabbath' (Matt. 12:11–12).

The Christian Sabbath

The fourth commandment stipulated that the Sabbath be kept on the seventh day of the week. Since the first century, however, Christians have observed and continue to observe the first day of the week as the Sabbath day—also known as 'the Lord's Day'. Something momentous must have happened to alter a commandment of God that was literally and metaphorically engraved in stone. That momentous event was the resurrection of Christ. It was 'on the first day of the week [that] Mary Magdalene came to the tomb early, while it was still dark' (John 20:1). It was 'after the sabbath, toward the dawn of the first day of the week, [that] Mary Magdalene and the other Mary went to see the sepulchre' (Matt. 28:1). Here they were greeted with the glorious news, 'Do not be afraid; for I know that you seek Jesus who was crucified. He is not here; for he has risen, as he said. Come, see the place where he lay' (Matt. 28:5–6).

The change of the Sabbath from the seventh to the first day of the week is one of the many compelling evidences that Christ really did rise from the dead. Only a momentous event could modify a commandment of God. Such an event was Christ's conquest of the grave: 'He was raised on the third day in accordance with the Scriptures' (1 Cor. 15:4). Christians have kept the first day of the week as their special day ever since. Acts 20:7 reveals, 'On the first day of the week, when we were gathered together to break bread, Paul talked with them.'

On the first day of the week Christians gather together in the presence of their risen Lord to worship God. They hear His Word explained and they pray to God the Father, through Christ, aided by the Holy Spirit. They also break bread and drink wine in memory of the Saviour's atoning death. They rejoice together in a common salvation procured by the One who died for their sins and was raised back to life again on the first day of the week. Sunday is thus the Christian's true 'holy day'. It is the Lord Jesus Christ who has made this day so exceedingly special. The Christian's Sunday is a foretaste of the eternal Sabbath of heaven above.

NOTE

1   Calvin, *Truth for All Time*, p. 15.

Festivals and feasts

C hristians are not generally known for their party-going. Christian qualms about parties have their root in a fear of undue worldliness, because the Lord calls us to be separate and distinct from the world (see Rom. 12:2). The people of God in Bible times, however, were not so inhibited when it came to partying. Their year was punctuated by various feasts and festivals. These are delineated in Leviticus 23 as 'the appointed feasts of the LORD' (v. 44). God commanded them to party! It is as if holy partying is as much a duty as holy praying. The feasts of Leviticus 23 kept the people's focus on the Lord and on His grace. With our New Testament hindsight, we can also see how they pictured and prefigured the coming of the Messiah and the salvation He would bring.

The Passover

The religious year began in April with the celebration of the 'Feast of the Passover'. The Passover feast commemorated God's delivering His people from slavery in Egypt. Central to the deliverance was the killing of an unblemished lamb and the application of its blood to the doorpost and lintel of the home. God's judgement of death passed through the whole land of Egypt, but God promised, 'when I see the blood, I will pass over you' (Exod. 12:13). The Israelites, then, were spared divine judgement—but only because of the blood of the lamb. God accepted the death of the lamb as a substitute. If a lamb had not been slain and its blood applied, that particular home experienced the death of its firstborn. When God's judgement fell on Egypt, the people of Israel were spared. This caused Pharaoh to act. With great urgency, he commanded the enslaved Israelites, 'Rise up, go forth from among my people' (Exod. 12:31). They were now free. They had been redeemed—and the Feast of the Passover was the annual celebration of this redemption.

The Passover feast was a joyful one. At the centre of the table was a roasted lamb. But they also ate bitter herbs—reminding them of their bitter slavery—and *haroset*—a sweet relish, reminding them of the mortar they had been forced to make as slaves. Unleavened bread was also eaten, for they left Egypt in haste, with no time to let their dough prove.

The Feast of the Passover pointed to a greater Lamb and a greater deliverance. Jesus came to deliver us from the 'Egypt' of sin and God's judgement. He did so by dying in our place and shedding His precious blood. The New Testament affirms, 'Christ, our paschal lamb, has been sacrificed' (1 Cor. 5:7) and 'In him we have redemption through his blood, the forgiveness of our trespasses, according to the riches of his grace' (Eph. 1:7).

The Feast of the First Fruits

'First Fruits' occurred 'on the morrow after the Sabbath' (Lev. 23:11) after the Passover—our Sunday. It marked the beginning of the spring wheat harvest, and the ritual stipulated, 'you shall bring the sheaf of the first fruits of your harvest to the priest; and he shall wave the sheaf before the LORD' (Lev. 23:10–11). The first sheaf of wheat was thus devoted to God. It symbolized that the whole harvest was actually His and implied that a fuller harvest was to follow.

'First fruits' gives us a remarkable picture of Christ. He died at Passover time 'like … a lamb without blemish or spot' (1 Peter 1:19) and 'on the morrow after the Sabbath'—the first day of the week—He was raised to life again. Paul proclaimed, 'Christ has been raised from the dead, the *first fruits* of those who have fallen asleep' (1 Cor. 15:20). As the full harvest followed the first sheaf, so, likewise, everyone united to Christ by faith will receive a new, glorious resurrection life at the last day. As Christ was raised to a new, glorious existence, so will His people be raised: 'Christ the first fruits, then at his coming those who belong to Christ' (1 Cor. 15:23). 'The Lord Jesus Christ ... will change our lowly body to be like his glorious body, by the power which enables him even to subject all things to himself' (Phil. 3:21).

Pentecost

Fifty days after Passover, 'the Feast of Weeks' occurred—also known as 'the Feast of Pentecost'. At this feast, two loaves were offered to God in celebration and thanksgiving at the end of the wheat harvest. The feast also commemorated the giving of the law on Mount Sinai fifty days after the first Passover. The law was a revelation of God's will, so the feast was also known as the 'Feast of Revelation'.

After the death, resurrection and ascension of Jesus, God poured out His Holy Spirit on the earth. And He did so at the Feast of Pentecost. It is the Holy Spirit of God who truly reveals God to us. He applies the saving work of Christ to our souls and makes Jesus real to us. His power within us also enables and empowers us to live lives pleasing to God—to keep His law. Pentecost was a kind of harvest festival. On *the* day of Pentecost there was a harvest of souls, as three thousand souls were saved through Peter's preaching of the redeeming, risen and reigning Christ (see Acts 2).

The Feast of Trumpets

This feast marked the beginning of the civil New Year. It occurred in our month of October, and it was so called because it was 'a memorial proclaimed with blast of trumpets' (Lev. 23:24).

Facing an unknown year can fill us with foreboding. The believer, however, may entrust all the unknown to a loving heavenly Father who knows all our unknowns. As our God is eternal, He is already in the future. He has predetermined the years we will live—'in thy book were written, every one of them, the days that were formed for me, when as yet there was none of them' (Ps. 139:16). We may trust His providential care as each day unfolds.

'Trumpets' also reminds us of the end of time, for, according to the Bible, the second coming of Christ will come with a trumpet blast: 'The Lord himself will descend from heaven with a cry of command, with the archangel's call, and with the sound of the trumpet of God' (1 Thes. 4:16). The trumpet will inaugurate our full salvation—our being raised to immortality: 'the trumpet will sound, and the dead will be raised imperishable, and we shall be changed' (1 Cor. 15:52).

The Day of Atonement

The annual 'Day of Atonement'—ten days after 'Trumpets'—was Israel's most solemn festival. It was not a feast but a fast. If fellowship with a holy God is to be enjoyed, sin has to be atoned for, or covered. At this festival, two goats were taken. One was sacrificed as the sinner's substitute—'the soul that sins shall die' (Ezek. 18:20). The other, however, was taken to the high priest, who laid his hand on its head and confessed the sins of the people over it, symbolically transferring those sins to the 'scapegoat'—the one who would take the blame for the people. The goat was then sent away into the wilderness, thus symbolically carrying the people's sins far away. Psalm 103:12 says, 'As far as the east is from the west, so far does he remove our transgressions from us.'

The Day of Atonement reached its fulfilment in Christ. The fact that the festival ritual was undertaken annually demonstrated that it could not permanently atone for sin. Jesus, however, does. He fulfils the role of the two goats in His one person. 'He has appeared once for all at the end of the age to put away sin by the sacrifice of himself' (Heb. 9:26). At Calvary He fully atoned for our sins. In an act of mercy, God imputed them to Him. He paid their price once and for all. If we belong to Jesus, our sins are forgiven and we have peace with God. 'We … rejoice in God through our Lord Jesus Christ, through whom we have now received our reconciliation' (Rom. 5:11).

The Feast of Tabernacles

The final feast of the year was the Feast of Booths or Tabernacles. This was celebrated in the autumn, during the fruit harvest. It was also known as 'Harvest' or 'Ingathering'. For this feast God commanded the people of Israel to 'take ... the fruit of goodly trees, branches of palm trees, and boughs of leafy trees, and willows of the brook; and ... rejoice before the LORD your God' (Lev. 23:40). The feast involved building a small tent or booth and living in it for the duration of the feast. This commemorated the time of Israel's wilderness wandering after the exodus, when they lived in tents for forty years, graciously sustained by the hand of God.

During the Feast of Tabernacles, the Jews prayed for the rain necessary for a good harvest, and with great ceremony, the high priest poured water from a golden ewer onto the horns of the altar. It was at that exact moment that Jesus gave the great invitation, 'If any one thirst, let him come to me and drink. He who believes in me, as the scripture has said, "Out of his heart shall flow rivers of living water"' (John 7:37–38).

'Tabernacles' pointed forward to Jesus. In Him, God dwelt in a 'tent'—a human body—and lived on this earth. 'The Word became flesh and dwelt among us, full of grace and truth' (John 1:14). 'Tabernacles' also points us forward to the consummation of our Christian salvation, when our fellowship with God will be unblemished, unhindered and unhandicapped by all our present impediments. At the glorious time it will be said,

Behold, the dwelling [tabernacle] of God is with men. He will dwell with them, and they shall be his people, and God himself will be with them; he will wipe away every tear from their eyes, and death shall be no more, neither shall there be mourning nor crying nor pain any more, for the former things have passed away (Rev. 21:3–4).

Hasten the day!

The vine

The land and climate of Bible times was ideal for growing grapes. These grapes, once harvested, could be eaten fresh, dried to make raisins or pressed to make wine. Vineyards abounded and still abound in the land of Israel.

When the twelve spies—one from each tribe—made their initial foray into the Promised Land of Canaan, during the time of Moses, Scripture records, 'they came to the Valley of Eshcol, and cut down from there a branch with a single cluster of grapes, and they carried it on a pole between two of them' (Num. 13:23). The name 'Eshcol' means 'cluster'.

The Lord Jesus once used the familiar imagery of the vineyard to tell a parable explaining His mission. The parable began, 'There was a householder who planted a vineyard, and set a hedge around it, and dug a wine press in it, and built a tower …' (Matt. 21:33). The scene would have resonated in the ears of His hearers:

- The *vineyard* would normally be located on a hillside where the grape clusters could catch the sun.
- The *hedge around it* was a fence of thorns, designed to deter wild animals who might damage the vintage, not to mention human thieves who might have the desire to raid the crop.
- The *wine press* was a rock cistern. Into this the grapes were put, and trodden by bare foot. Ropes overhead prevented those treading the grapes from slipping. When the grapes were trodden, the juice ran out of the main cistern through channels into a lower cistern. Here the sediment was allowed to settle and the grape juice collected into vats. This was fermented, and then poured into smaller vessels. The vessels were sealed, but had a small hole enabling gases to be released during the final stages of fermentation.

Sometimes this wine was put into leather bottles. If the leather was old and brittle, the gases released by fermentation might burst the bottle. This is the background to Jesus' words, 'No one puts new wine into old wineskins; if he does, the new wine will burst the skins and it will be spilled, and the skins will be destroyed. But new wine must be put into fresh wineskins' (Luke 5:37–38).

- A *tower* was built for security purposes—to look out for thieves during the harvest. If a tower was too costly to build, a tent would suffice. During the grape-harvesting season a whole extended family might move into this tent.

God's vine

Interestingly, the people of God in Old Testament times were represented by the symbol of the vine. They were to be a plantation of God for His glory. Thus we read in Psalm 80:8–9, 'Thou didst bring a vine out of Egypt; thou didst drive out the nations and plant it. Thou didst clear the ground for it; it took deep root and filled the land.' Similarly, in Isaiah 5:7 we read, 'For the vineyard of the LORD of hosts is the house of Israel, and the men of Judah are his pleasant planting.' Sadly, however, the Old Testament reveals that God's vine did not always live up to its divine calling: 'He looked for it to yield grapes, but it yielded wild grapes … he looked for justice, but behold, bloodshed; for righteousness, but behold, a cry!' (Isa. 5:2, 7). God's vine was designed to yield the fruit of undivided devotion and obedience to Him. The reality, though, was somewhat different …

The true vine

It is against the above background of a disappointing vintage that we understand Jesus' claim in John 15:1: 'I am the true vine, and my Father is the vinedresser.' Whereas Israel failed, the Lord Jesus succeeded, for He is 'the true vine'. God the Father said of Him, 'This is my beloved Son, with whom I am well pleased' (Matt. 3:17). The Lord Jesus then went on to explain the secret of a fruitful Christian life—how we may bear fruit to the glory of God. The secret is abiding in Jesus, having a living union and communion with Him—knowing His Holy Spirit living and working in and through us. Jesus said,

Abide in me, and I in you. As the branch cannot bear fruit by itself, unless it abides in the vine, neither can you, unless you abide in me. I am the vine, you are the branches. He who abides in me, and I in him, he it is that bears much fruit, for apart from me you can do nothing (John 15:4–5).

Scripture describes the relationship between the Christian and the Saviour in various complementary ways. For example, He is our Head. We are the parts of His body, vitally connected to Him. Here, though, we see that He is the vine, and we are the branches on which the grapes grow. Branches cannot bear fruit unless sap from the main vine flows into them. There is a vital connection between the branches and the main vine. Similarly, we cannot bear fruit unless we abide in Christ, 'the true vine'. We have to be vitally connected to Him in a living, loving union.

The Lord Jesus was obviously well acquainted with horticultural practice. John 15 reveals that He knew that branches on a vine were pruned each spring. This was so that the plant's energy was channelled into producing the maximum amount of fruit and not dead wood. Jesus likened God the Father to an expert vinedresser: 'I am the true vine, and my Father is the vinedresser … every branch that does bear fruit he prunes, that it may bear more fruit' (John 15:1–2). Here we have a window into the sufferings we often experience in this life. God the Father lovingly exercises His pruning hook on His children. He cuts away all that hinders our fruitfulness. He applies a sharp knife to all who are united to Jesus, 'the true vine'. The process is painful, but it produces wonderful results. It produces fruit to the glory of God. It results in a closer walk with Him and a deeper dependence on Him. It produces human sympathy and tenderness, godly character and greater Christ-likeness in us. 'By this my Father is glorified, that you bear much fruit' (John 15:8). Martin Luther once said, 'I have had two main teachers in my life. The Scriptures and my sufferings.'

The final harvest

Finally, and formidably, we note that the imagery of the wine press and the process of treading grapes is employed in the Bible to direct our attention to the final judgement at the end of the age. Grape juice can be blood red. The book of Revelation describes the time on God's calendar when all those outside of Christ will be put into God's wine press and judged. The language employed in Revelation is highly symbolic, and yet it describes an event which will be realer than real, and more horrific than any words can describe. A command will be issued:

'Put in your sickle, and gather the clusters of the vine of the earth, for its grapes are ripe.' So the angel swung his sickle on the earth and gathered the vintage of the earth, and threw it into the great wine press of the wrath of God; and the wine press was trodden outside the city, and the blood flowed from the wine press (Rev. 14:18–20).

The 'wine press of the wrath of God' is the most fearsome reality of all. If it were not for the wrath of God against sinners, we would have no need of the gospel. It is the wrath of God which gives the gospel its imperative, which is 'flee from the wrath to come' (Matt. 3:7). The gospel is the only means by which we may be delivered from the wrath of God. The gospel is focused on the cross of Christ, where He endured the wrath of God in the sinner's place. If we belong to Jesus, we are both saved and safe:

Since, therefore, we are now justified by his blood, much more shall we be saved by him from the wrath of God (Rom. 5:9).

Jesus ... delivers us from the wrath to come (1 Thes. 1:10).

Jesus Himself gave the promise:

Truly, truly, I say to you, he who hears my word and believes him who sent me, has eternal life; he does not come into judgment but has passed from death to life (John 5:24).

Sitting by the city gate

'Our feet have been standing within your gates, O Jerusalem!' recalled the psalmist (Ps. 122:2). The walled city of Jerusalem is punctuated by huge gates. In Bible times, these gates were shut at night, when the night watchmen began their night watch on the walls. Latecomers could only gain entrance to the city through a small side gate, once the gatekeeper had ascertained their identity. At the end of their night shift, the watchmen would look for the 'morning star' to appear in the sky. This 'dayspring' would usher in the dawn. Hence Psalm 130:6: 'My soul waits for the LORD more than watchmen for the morning.' As the gates were large, so the keys which opened and locked them were also large. All this gives point to some of the claims of Jesus. The gospel proclaims that He can open the gate of eternal life to us, for He is 'the holy one, the true one, who has the key of David, who opens and no one shall shut, who shuts and no one opens' (Rev. 3:7). A gate key signified authority. Jesus has divine authority to bestow eternal life.

In Bible times, the city gate was a social hub. Here people met to hear the gossip. Here business transactions were negotiated. And here the elders responsible for running the city sat. People would come to them to resolve disputes. Suffering Job might well have been one such elder, for he recalled how 'when I went out to the gate of the city, when I prepared my seat in the square, the young men saw me and withdrew, and the aged rose and stood' (Job 29:7–8).

If we had taken a seat at the city gate in Bible times—perhaps the Damascus Gate—and viewed the proceedings for an hour, we would have noticed that 'all life is there'. We would have seen various occupations and factions of people, including:

A water-seller

The water-seller's services would have been partaken of gladly in Bible times, in the hot Middle East. Household water, pumped through the mains and obtained 'on tap', was unknown then. You would, however, have to pay the water-seller for his goods and service. This contrasts with the closing gospel invitation and promise of the Bible: 'Let him who is thirsty come, let him who desires take the water of life without price' (Rev. 22:17). The Christian gospel is a gospel of free grace.

A burden-bearer

Heavy loads, in Bible times, would be carried by a professional burden-bearer. His tool of trade was just a knotted rope. Once inside the city, it was impractical for animals to carry loads up the steeply stepped alley ways. The burden-bearer would do this, his veins bulging as he did so.

Scripture teaches that the greatest burden-bearer of all is the Lord Jesus Christ. He still gives the invitation, 'Come to me, all who labor and are heavy laden, and I will give you rest' (Matt. 11:28). Our sin is the greatest burden which we carry. The psalmist spoke for us all when he said, 'my iniquities have gone over my head; they weigh like a burden too heavy for me' (Ps. 38:4). Jesus alone is able to remove our burden of sin. 'He himself bore our sins in his body on the tree' (1 Peter 2:24).

The forerunner

In Bible times, an important person—for example, the Roman governor or the high priest—would be preceded by a forerunner. The forerunner would 'pave the way' for his master, alerting people to his presence, getting people out of his way, opening doors for him and responding to every movement of his eyes and hands. The forerunner would have a wooden club in his hand and would not be averse to using it should someone get in the way. He would shout, 'Make way! Make way!'

The Lord Jesus had a forerunner. Scripture predicted, 'Behold, I will send you Elijah the prophet before the great and terrible day of the LORD comes' (Mal. 4:5). The prophecy was fulfilled in the Elijah-type figure of John the Baptist, who explained, 'I am the voice of one crying in the wilderness, "Make straight the way of the Lord"' (John 1:23).

Amazingly, Scripture describes the Lord Jesus Himself as 'a forerunner on our behalf' (Heb. 6:20). He has gone before us into heaven. His death on the cross for our sins has made us fit for heaven. In heaven, He is currently preparing a home for us (John 14:1–2). Jesus, our divine Forerunner, has paved the way for our eternal salvation!

A Roman soldier

The ubiquitous Roman soldier was a certain sight in first-century Jerusalem. Israel was an occupied country. The Roman soldier's presence was resented by many, but, on the positive side, it helped to keep the peace. If the soldier was feeling vindictive, he could commandeer you to carry his pack. You would not say no! This underlies Jesus' words, 'If any one forces you to go one mile, go with him two miles' (Matt. 5:41). He was saying that we should reflect the character of God, as He is kind to the undeserving and unworthy, and gives us far more than we could ever deserve.

The Zealots

The Zealots, however, were all for taking the law into their own hands and getting rid of the Romans by military force. It is possible that two of Jesus' disciples—Simon the Zealot and Judas Iscariot—either belonged to the Zealot party or were sympathetic to their aims. They were unable to recruit the Lord Jesus to their ranks, however. He defined His mission in spiritual, not military or political, terms. No sooner had Peter confessed Jesus to be the longed-for Messiah than Jesus 'began to show his disciples that he must go to Jerusalem and suffer many things … and be killed, and on the third day be raised' (Matt. 16:21). The central symbol of the Christian faith is not a sword but a cross. 'Christ Jesus came into the world to save sinners' (1 Tim. 1:15).

Beggars

Beggars were as common in Bible times as they are in our cities today. In Bible times there was no state benefit, so those who hit hard times were dependent on the mercy of others. The law of Moses was highly compassionate here, for it stipulated,

If there is among you a poor man, one of your brethren, in any of your towns within your land which the LORD your God gives you, you shall not harden your heart or shut your hand against your poor brother, but you shall open your hand to him, and lend him sufficient for his need, whatever it may be (Deut. 15:7–8).

The Pharisees

The Pharisees were the largest religious group in the time of the Lord Jesus. Their name means 'the separated ones'. They were very strict—even overly strict—in their obedience to the law of Moses. This led at times to legalism, self-righteousness and a tendency to look down on those they considered not to be in their league. Some Pharisees, however—notably Nicodemus and Saul of Tarsus—came to know and love the Lord Jesus Christ.

The Sadducees

The Sadducees were similar to the Pharisees. Unlike them, however, they did not accept the oral law, but only the written law. They accepted only the first five books of the Bible and denied the resurrection of the body. Coming from the families of the priests who ministered in the temple, they tended to be aristocratic in their ways and people of means. They claimed to be descended from Zadok the priest, and had much more power and influence than the Pharisees. Their friendship with the Roman rulers made them suspect in the eyes of the people. The Pharisees and Sadducees together formed the Sanhedrin—the highest religious and judicial authority of the Jewish people at the time of Christ.

The Saviour of the world

Would we have seen the Lord Jesus in Jerusalem in the first century? Only if we had been in the right place at the right time. What a privilege it would have been, for to see Jesus is to see God. He could say, 'He who has seen me has seen the Father' (John 14:9). 'He is the image of the invisible God' (Col. 1:15). The question is irrelevant, as God has put us where we are, to work out our salvation in the particular circumstances He has ordained for us. If our faith is in Christ, however, we will surely see Him one day! Scripture says of all whose faith is in Jesus that 'they shall see his face' (Rev. 22:4). Although we have never seen Jesus in this life, we will most surely see Him in the next. The glory of heaven and the joy of salvation is Jesus Himself. The Christian will enjoy His blessed company for all eternity, in the city of the New Jerusalem.

When all my labours and trials are o'er,
And I am safe on that beautiful shore,
Just to be near the dear Lord I adore
Will through the ages be glory for me.

Oh, that will be glory for me,
Glory for me, glory for me,
When by His grace I shall look on His face,
That will be glory, be glory for me.

When by the gift of His infinite grace,
I am accorded in heaven a place,

Chapter 22

Just to be there and to look on His face
Will through the ages be glory for me.[1]

Soli Deo Gloria.

NOTE

1   Charles H. Gabriel, 'When All My Labours and Trials Are O'er'.